Long Key

UNIVERSITY PRESS OF FLORIDA

Florida A&M University, Tallahassee
Florida Atlantic University, Boca Raton
Florida Gulf Coast University, Ft. Myers
Florida International University, Miami
Florida State University, Tallahassee
New College of Florida, Sarasota
University of Central Florida, Orlando
University of Florida, Gainesville
University of North Florida, Jacksonville
University of South Florida, Tampa
University of West Florida, Pensacola

UNIVERSITY PRESS
OF FLORIDA

Gainesville ▪ Tallahassee ▪ Tampa
Boca Raton ▪ Pensacola ▪ Orlando ▪ Miami
Jacksonville ▪ Ft. Myers ▪ Sarasota

LONG KEY

Flagler's Island Getaway for the Rich and Famous

THOMAS NEIL
KNOWLES

Printed in the United States of America
on recycled, acid-free paper

This book may be available in an electronic edition.

19 18 17 16 15 14 6 5 4 3 2 1

Library of Congress Cataloging-in-Publication Data
Knowles, Thomas Neil. author.
Long Key : Flagler's island getaway for the rich and
famous / Thomas Neil Knowles.
pages cm
Includes bibliographical references and index.
ISBN 978-0-8130-4976-2
1. Flagler, Henry Morrison, 1830–1913. 2. Layton (Fla.)—History.
3. Long Key Fishing Club (Fla.)—History. 4. Florida Keys (Fla.)—
History. 5. Florida East Coast Railway—History. I. Title.
F319.L29K66 2014
975.9'41—dc23
2013038962

The University Press of Florida is the scholarly publishing agency for the State University System of Florida, comprising Florida A&M University, Florida Atlantic University, Florida Gulf Coast University, Florida International University, Florida State University, New College of Florida, University of Central Florida, University of Florida, University of North Florida, University of South Florida, and University of West Florida.

UNIVERSITY PRESS OF FLORIDA
15 Northwest 15th Street
Gainesville, FL 32611-2079
http://www.upf.com

In remembrance of my grandfather, Thomas Milton Knowles, a Key West charter-boat captain, and my father, Neil Milton Knowles, both of whom knew not only the names of the fishes of the Florida Keys, but also their addresses and dining preferences.

Contents

Preface

Beginning in 1888 and continuing through the first decade of the twentieth century, Henry Flagler opened nine resorts along Florida's east coast from St. Augustine to the Florida Keys and two in the Bahamas. Most of his resorts were characterized by a large, elegant structure with the table, service, manicured grounds, and ancillary facilities and accoutrements expected of a first-class hotel. The eleventh and last of the Flagler resorts to be opened during his lifetime was radically different in appearance and more casual in operation than its predecessors. The unpretentiously named Long Key Fishing Camp attracted a diverse and notable clientele ranging from aristocrats and nobility to writers and poets, and fostered among its guests an unparalleled level of camaraderie and loyalty.

Much has been written about the palatial resorts Flagler built, but the Long Key Fishing Camp has languished in obscurity ever since it was destroyed by the 1935 Labor Day Hurricane. This historical account seeks to fill this void by bringing together material from many sources to provide a comprehensive record of the resort flavored with some of the experiences of individuals who were involved with it.

Especially important to this endeavor are the recollections of and materials provided by Patricia Duane, the daughter of James Duane, caretaker of the camp during the five years preceding its destruction. Although she was a child during that period, her remarkable recall and her willingness to share her memories as well as her collection of photographs and other materials have significantly enhanced this work.

Both the railroad to Key West and the Long Key Fishing Camp were destroyed by the same powerful hurricane. It was the first hurricane making landfall in the United States to be classified by government meteorologists as a category-5 storm, the most catastrophic designation on the Saffir-Simpson Hurricane Wind Scale. The discussion of this calamitous event has been limited in this work in order to maintain the focus on Long Key. A comprehensive account of the hurricane and its impact on the Florida Keys will be found in my 2009 book, *Category 5: The 1935 Labor Day Hurricane.*

Any discussion of Henry Flagler's activities in Florida would be incomplete without reference to the sums of money involved. In this book, unless otherwise noted, monetary amounts are expressed in dollar values applicable to the period being discussed. Where equivalent dollars are stated, the values were obtained from MeasuringWorth.com using the Historic Standard of Living with 2012 as the current year, the latest year for which the requisite Consumer Price Index averages were available.

Most of Flagler's Florida hotels, including the Long Key Fishing Camp, were operational only during the winter months. The costs of a stay were high, and only the wealthy could afford regular visits. This observation caused me to wonder how many wealthy people lived in the United States while Flagler was engaged in his Florida enterprise. The answer seemed to be a fitting place to begin this work.

Prologue

The Top 0.006 Percent

Sixty years ago there were no great fortunes in America, few large fortunes, and no poverty. Now there is some poverty (though few places can it be called pauperism), many large fortunes, and a greater number of gigantic fortunes than in any other country of the world.

—James Bryce, *The American Commonwealth*, 1889

John Jacob Astor was the wealthiest man in the United States when he died in 1848. At that time there were only fifty people living in the country with assets worth $1 million; Astor's estate was valued at twenty times that. Forty-four years later, after conducting an eighteen-month survey, the *New York Tribune* published the names and cities of residence of 4,047 people in the United States reputed to be worth $1 million or more. The purchasing power of $1 million in 1892 was approximately equivalent to $26 million in 2012.[1]

The survey relied heavily on subjective estimates and was politically motivated; however, the data provide some insight into the distribution of personal wealth and where the wealthiest people lived. Using the *Tribune* data and population figures from the 1890 U.S. Census yields the following tidbits.

- One out of every 15,562 inhabitants of the United States (.00642 percent) was a millionaire.
- Three-fourths of America's wealthiest people lived in seven of the forty-four states: New York (1,508); Pennsylvania (379); Illinois (316); Maryland (296); Ohio (207); California (192); and New Jersey (124).

- The remaining 1,025 millionaires were scattered over thirty-four other states; none were reported to be residing in Kansas, Nevada, and South Dakota.
- The largest concentration of the wealthy was in New York City, where there were 1,100 millionaires, one for every 1,374 residents.

In addition to the millionaires identified by the *Tribune*, another source estimates that there were two hundred people who had tens of millions and six who had hundreds of millions in 1892.

The population of people having $1 million or more in the United States remained fairly level through the first decade of the twentieth century and then began to increase, reaching 10,000 in 1918 and 20,000 eleven years later on the eve of the Great Depression.[2]

Many factors led to the extraordinary growth of wealth in the United States during the latter half of the nineteenth century. Immigration caused the population to swell dramatically, providing a pool of laborers and skilled craftsmen as well as more consumers. The rapid expansion of railroads and telegraph systems vastly improved transportation and communications. Discoveries of domestic deposits of valuable natural resources including gold, silver, iron ore, coal, and petroleum, and the development of better techniques for extracting and refining them provided raw materials and lucrative investment opportunities.

American entrepreneurs began to innovate new ways of organizing capital ventures and manipulating markets. Those who recognized opportunities and took aggressive action were richly rewarded.

Astor was one of the earliest of a class of businessmen in the United States for whom the goal was not merely to become wealthy, but to become powerful enough to take control of a given market by eliminating competitors. Industrial espionage, secret agreements for rebates, and the enactment of tariffs and statutes that stifled competition were considered to be tools of the trade in this monopolistic arena. The concept of controlling a product from the source of raw materials to the distribution of the finished item was deployed whenever possible. The most successful of these manipulators grew enormously wealthy, ultimately at the expense of the consumer. They controlled production, set the price, and even decreed who could sell their products, all the while using false-front companies controlled by corporate headquarters to maintain the appearance of competition.

Antimonopoly movements became especially critical in the 1880s of the men who reaped extraordinary profits from such predatory practices. The most aggressive of these were vilified as extortionists disguised as businessmen and labeled "robber barons" after the medieval barons who erected forts and barriers along the Rhine River in Europe and exacted exorbitant tolls to allow merchants' barges to pass or robbed them outright.[3]

During the late nineteenth and early twentieth centuries, this unflattering title was bestowed on some of the richest men in America including Andrew Carnegie, Charles M. Schwab, Henry Clay Frick, J. P. Morgan, Jay Gould, Edward Henry Harriman, John D. Rockefeller, and Henry Morrison Flagler. Carnegie, Schwab, and Frick made their fortunes in steel. Morgan garnered his wealth in finance and industrial consolidation. Gould and Harriman made their millions in railroads.

Rockefeller and Flagler were partners in the refining and transportation of oil during the industry's formative years. They founded the Standard Oil Company and aggressively guided it to a dominant position in the world market as demand for petroleum products soared, first as an inexpensive replacement for whale oil for artificial lighting and then as fuels and lubricants for internal-combustion engines. Rockefeller became the first American billionaire. Henry Flagler did not amass nearly as great a fortune as his partner, primarily because he did not own as much of Standard Oil as Rockefeller, but when he died in 1913, his estate was valued at $75 million.[4]

His net worth would have been much greater had he stayed in New York, but Henry Flagler chose to spend the last twenty-eight years of his life personally overseeing and funding the development of what was then commonly regarded as a primitive land, Florida's east coast. Four years before he died, Flagler said wryly, "If it wasn't for Florida, I'd be quite a rich man today." Why would he risk his fortune and invest so heavily in such a costly venture so late in life?[5]

By 1909 Henry Flagler's investments in Florida amounted to $41 million, comprising $18 million in railroads on the mainland, $10 million in the railroad being constructed from the mainland to Key West, $12 million in hotels, and $1 million in steamboat and other enterprises (*Banker's Magazine*, February 1909).

1

Why Did Henry Do It?

> And still, in all the golden floods that were washing around him from Standard Oil, Mr. Flagler never forgot his boyhood's dream. He still wanted to keep a hotel. But his ambitions had broadened since his early visions at Canandaigua. He would have been satisfied then with a plain little country tavern, where the village oracles could prop their feet on the fender around the office stove and talk about Henry Clay's chances for the presidency. Now he wanted to be among hotelkeepers what the Standard Oil Company was among corporations. He could not be comfortable anywhere but at the top.
>
> —Samuel E. Moffett, "Henry Morrison Flagler"

Henry Flagler experienced poverty twice in his life, the first time by circumstance of birth, the second time when he made a bad investment. He was born in 1830 in Hopewell, New York. His father was an itinerant country preacher whose income was low and sporadic due to his penchant for going off on temperance and other missions. At age fourteen, Henry left home to ease the family's financial burden and worked his way to a small Ohio town near Cleveland. There he began his professional life as an assistant in a general store.[1]

With hard work, an eighth-grade education, and an innate business savvy, he worked his way up. By the time he was twenty-two he had saved enough to become a partner in a venture to build a distillery to make liquor for railroad workers. During the next three years Henry married, fathered a daughter, and made a modest fortune. He also met and became friends with an ambitious grain salesman named John Rockefeller.[2]

When the unrest preceding the Civil War escalated and salt prices rose dramatically, Flagler saw an opportunity to expand his wealth. He sold all of his business interests and invested the proceeds and his savings, a total of one hundred thousand dollars, in a salt-production plant in Michigan. The plant manufactured salt by extracting brine from the remnants of a primeval sea trapped beneath the Lower Peninsula of Michigan. The elevated salt prices and relatively low entry costs of salt extraction lured many others to start up similar companies. The result was cutthroat competition and uncontrolled production. As the amount of salt on the market increased, the commodity's price declined and Flagler's profits dwindled. Salt prices plummeted when the Civil War ended, and Flagler's company went bankrupt.

Henry lost his entire investment and owed his workers fifty thousand dollars in wages. He borrowed funds to pay off his employees, but for a while he was so destitute that he did not eat regularly so that his family had enough to eat. He finally found work as a salesman on a commission basis for a grain merchant in Cleveland. He did well and made speculative investments. Within two years, he had enough money to pay off his loan and buy the grain merchant's business.

While Flagler had been in Michigan, John Rockefeller had become involved with a small oil-refining business. Around the mid-1800s, it had been found that distilling crude oil could produce kerosene, a fuel for lamps superior to expensive whale oil. Demand for the kerosene was great, but production was limited by the small quantities of crude available. At that time crude oil was harvested by skimming the surface of ponds and streams where natural seepage occurred. The subsequent discovery of significant subsurface oil deposits in northwestern Pennsylvania coupled with the development of effective drilling and pumping techniques dramatically improved the supply of crude. The petroleum business in the United States was poised to become a major industry.

Rockefeller, an amazingly successful entrepreneur, was eager to expand and upgrade his oil-refinery venture but needed capital and began looking for partners. Impressed with Flagler's business prowess and his ability to recover so quickly from financial disaster, Rockefeller sought him out: "When the oil business was developing and we needed more help, I at once thought of Mr. Flagler as a possible partner, and made him an offer to come with us and give up his commission business. This offer he accepted, and so began that life-long friendship which has never had a moment's interruption."[3]

In 1867 Rockefeller and Flagler with several other partners established a new oil-refining company in Cleveland, Ohio. Because a basic distillation plant could be set up with a modest investment, refineries were sprouting up everywhere, and the specter of uncontrolled production that had ruined Flagler's salt business in Michigan threatened to do the same for the refining industry in Cleveland. Rockefeller and Flagler recognized this threat from the outset and made their plans accordingly. They immediately began to arrange secret rebates from the railroads that transported oil and took other actions that gave their company an advantage over the competition. When rivals floundered they were either acquired at a bargain price or forced out of business. Within two years Rockefeller and Flagler refineries had the largest capacity in the world.

In 1870, at Flagler's suggestion, they incorporated their business. Though Flagler had no formal legal training, he drew up the articles of incorporation creating the Standard Oil Company with Rockefeller, the largest shareholder, as president.

They made a very effective business team; Rockefeller with his acuity with numbers and Flagler with his natural ability to succinctly translate business arrangements into contractual and other legal documents. Rockefeller was so impressed with his colleague's legal prowess that he noted in his memoirs: "Mr. Flagler drew practically all our contracts. He has always had the faculty of being able to clearly express the intent and purpose of a contract so well and accurately that there could be no misunderstanding, and his contracts were fair to both sides."

By 1872 Standard Oil controlled most of the refineries in Cleveland. Six years later the company controlled the majority of refining capacity in all major American refining cities. Rockefeller's holdings in Standard Oil in 1879 were worth $18 million; Flagler's were valued at $6 million. Both men invested their profits wisely, and their personal fortunes grew.[4]

Crude oil was transported in barrels by railroads and drayage companies during the early days of the industry. Later, pipelines were laid from the oil fields direct to the refineries, moving the oil much more efficiently and at a substantially reduced cost. Standard Oil began acquiring pipeline companies and by 1884 had effectively monopolized the transportation of crude oil in the United States.

Significant changes took place in Henry Flagler's personal life during the

1880s. His wife of eighteen years died in 1881 of a progressive lung ailment. He married again in 1883 and late in that year took his wife to St. Augustine, Florida. The announced purpose of the trip was for a vacation, but Flagler also wanted to pursue a hunch that Florida in general, and the nation's oldest city in particular, had great potential as a resort destination.

He had been there eight years earlier with his first wife in the hope that a more moderate climate would be beneficial for her respiratory condition, but the accommodations had been so terrible that they went back to Jacksonville and shortened their visit. On this second visit the Flaglers stayed at a new hotel at St. Augustine and were so pleased with the service and rooms that they stayed through the winter. Henry's hunch began to change into a strategy.

After eighteen years of very demanding work in the oil business, Flagler was ready for a change in his professional life. He was already financially independent, the income from Standard Oil and other investments having made him a millionaire many times over. He retired from his management position and became a member of Standard Oil's board of directors. John Rockefeller was not surprised at his friend's actions and wrote that, "It was to be expected of such a man that he should fulfill his destiny by working out some great problems at a time when most men want to retire to a comfortable life of ease."[5]

Henry returned to St. Augustine in February 1885 and initiated the building of a world-class hotel, the Ponce de Leon. Within three years Flagler had built two hotels, the Ponce de Leon and the Alcazar, and was remodeling another he had purchased, the Cordova, all in St. Augustine. He had also bought and upgraded a short-line railroad to transport construction materials and hotel guests from Jacksonville. The rapidity with which he committed his personal wealth to a business in which he had no prior professional experience baffled his colleagues in the Northeast. Most puzzling of all was the location: Why St. Augustine, a place primarily known as a sanatorium where the infirm sought the alleged restorative powers of the climate?

Flagler said simply that the city appealed to him, and while its hotels had improved, there was little to do for recreation and amusement other than taking walks around the city. He believed someone with "sufficient means" should build a first-class hotel that not only offered a place to sleep and eat, but could also provide multiple venues where active people with plenty of money could spend it doing things they enjoy. Florida had the climate and natural beauty; Flagler provided the facilities and organization that allowed people of means to experience it in comfort and style.[6]

The lavish Ponce de Leon was, for a time, the finest and most expensive hotel in Florida. Advertised as having 450 rooms, the hotel occupied an entire city block. The exterior walls of poured concrete were sculpted to look like a Spanish palace, a theme reinforced throughout the guest areas by the liberal use of the finest materials such as marble from Africa and ornate décor including bronze seashell doorknobs.

In the lobby and other public areas, massive sculpted oak columns supported soaring ceilings covered with masterful murals that formed a colorful background for the glittering chandeliers. Elevators moved guests among the floors of the four-story structure, and thousands of electric lights highlighted the interior and exterior ornamentation. Service was impeccable throughout.[7]

Travel guides announced that the dining room/ballroom could accommodate eight hundred people and had musical balconies at each end for orchestras; newspapers extensively covered the elaborate dances and costume balls staged therein. Guests could enjoy a quiet walk around the fabulous gardens on the grounds, or the staff could arrange fishing trips, tours, and other diversions. If one had the money, there was no finer facility in the United States where it could be so satisfactorily spent.[8]

Flagler relished his new role as developer in a land where the changes he made had an immediate physical and economic impact that seemed to be welcomed by most of the general populace. The hotels, train service, and municipal improvements he brought to St. Augustine were a great success, and the former robber baron was sought out, even courted, to expand his railroad and resorts farther south. The St. Augustine experience set the pattern for Flagler's mode of operation for the next two decades. He acquired more small railroads, improved and consolidated them, and then extended the line down the east coast of Florida, building hotels and even towns along the way to create destinations that would attract travelers and settlers.

The works Flagler orchestrated in Florida were on a scale so prodigious that even John Rockefeller was impressed. Rockefeller wrote, "This one man, by his own energy and capital, has opened up a vast stretch of country, so that the old inhabitants and the new settlers may have a market for their products. He has given work to thousands of these people; and, to crown all, he has undertaken and nearly completed a remarkable engineering feat in carrying his road on the Florida Keys into the Atlantic Ocean to Key West, the point set out for years ago."[9]

This exhibit of lavish Flagler hotels appeared in a 1912 pamphlet formally announcing the opening of the Key West Extension. The Long Key Fishing Camp is conspicuously absent from this display. Courtesy of the Wright Langley Archives.

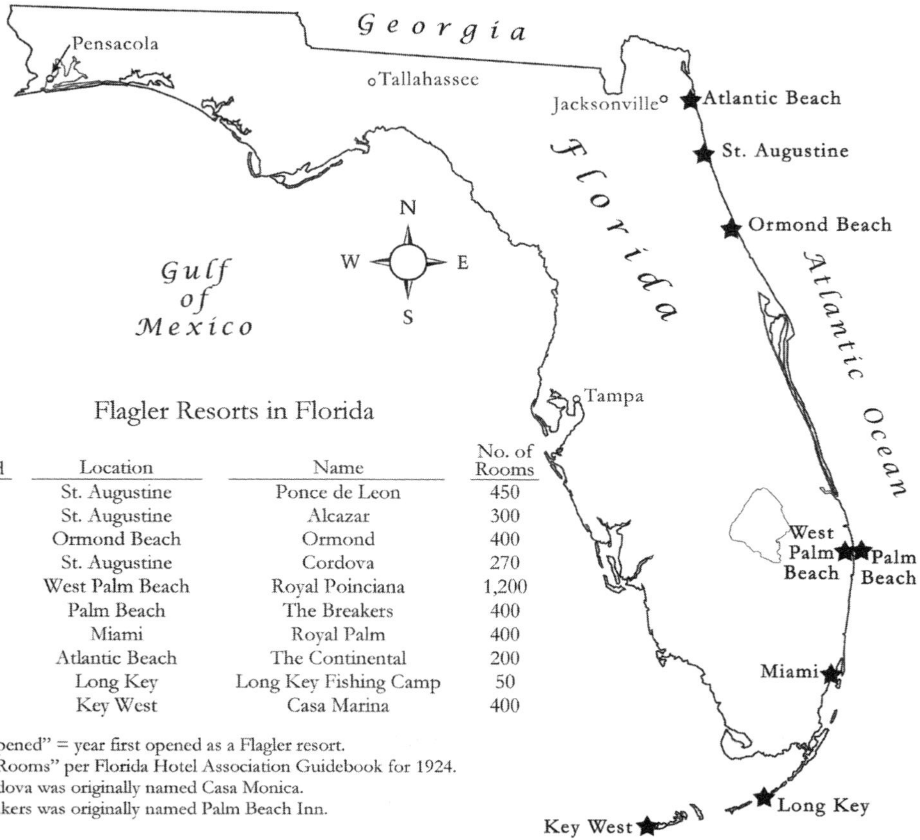

Flagler Resorts in Florida

Year Opened	Location	Name	No. of Rooms
1888	St. Augustine	Ponce de Leon	450
1888	St. Augustine	Alcazar	300
1889	Ormond Beach	Ormond	400
1894	St. Augustine	Cordova	270
1894	West Palm Beach	Royal Poinciana	1,200
1896	Palm Beach	The Breakers	400
1897	Miami	Royal Palm	400
1901	Atlantic Beach	The Continental	200
1908	Long Key	Long Key Fishing Camp	50
1921	Key West	Casa Marina	400

Notes:
"Year Opened" = year first opened as a Flagler resort.
"No. of Rooms" per Florida Hotel Association Guidebook for 1924.
The Cordova was originally named Casa Monica.
The Breakers was originally named Palm Beach Inn.

Flagler's resorts in Florida, 1921. By the second decade of the twentieth century, Flagler's resorts spanned the length of the Florida peninsula. Map by Thomas Neil Knowles.

2

The Oversea Railroad, Long Key, and the Viaduct

The dinner, which was served shortly before sunset, was a veritable feast. On its bill of fare appeared oysters, green turtle soup, fish chowder, turtle steaks, baked kingfish, stewed ducks, roasted 'possum, a variety of canned vegetables, an immense plum duff, canned fruits, crackers, cheese, and coffee; while the whole was seasoned with the sauce of hearty appetites and capital digestions. It was a substantial meal, as well as a merry one, and it gave Worth Manton a new insight into the possibilities of life on the Florida Keys.

—Kirk Munroe, *Canoemates*

The building of a railroad from the Florida mainland to Key West early in the twentieth century was a massive undertaking. Known as the "Island City," Key West was the most populous city in Florida from 1820 until 1890. Connecting it to the mainland via railroad had been discussed for more than fifty years.

The economic motivation for a rail link was the financial gain to be realized by speeding the movement of fruit and other perishable products from Cuba and Central America to lucrative northern markets in the United States. The transit time required by ships to reach existing U.S. ports served by railroads left little margin for delays caused by weather or other problems. Even when all went well, diminished product quality from spoilage was rampant. The use of harvested or manufactured ice to reduce these losses was impractical due to the procurement cost and the cargo capacity lost to stowage of the large, frozen blocks. Refrigeration equipment was in its infancy during the early 1900s, and practical shipboard installations were yet to come. As railroads expanded across the Florida peninsula, Key West—with its natural, deepwater harbor and close proximity to Cuba and Central America—became ever more attractive as a major transfer terminal.

Commencing in 1902, Flagler had a team of engineers survey possible routes for a rail line to Key West. The project would eventually involve construction at multiple work sites, including remote islands surrounded by shallow water; bridging over several deepwater channels; and the management and support of thousands of workers scattered over 100 miles, all occurring in an area prone to hurricanes and requiring more than a decade to complete. There was doubt that the project could even be done with the equipment, materials, and engineering skills available at the time. It took two years to find the answer.

By 1904 the Florida East Coast Railway had been extended southwest from Miami into an area that had become known as homestead country because most of the fertile land was owned by the U.S. government and was available for homesteading. The 30-mile rail line was built to tap the freight traffic generated by packinghouses handling the produce of farms in the area, and to provide a point from which the line could be extended to Key West should the decision be made to do so. At its terminus, a small town was laid out and a station built along with a wye junction that allowed trains to be turned around without a turntable. The town became known as Homestead. Fewer than 20 miles to the southeast lay the Florida Keys.

Flagler did not ask if extending the line to Key West could be done at a cost that would make the venture profitable. He just wanted to know if it could be built. Receiving an affirmative response, the seventy-four-year-old man simply said, "Very well, then go ahead. Go to Key West." Within weeks surveyors began staking the route across 19 swampy miles of the Everglades, then over twenty-nine islands on the eastern edge of Florida Bay and across forty-three intervening bodies of water.[1]

Midway down the Florida Keys, the surveyors came to an island with the distinctive shape of a snake's head in profile with wide-open jaws facing northeast and the stub of a neck pointing southwest. Early Spanish cartographers labeled it with names such as Cayo Vivora (Rattlesnake Key) and Cayo Bivoras (Vipers Key). The reptilian association faded away during the early 1800s, and the name changed to Long Island and then Long Key.[2]

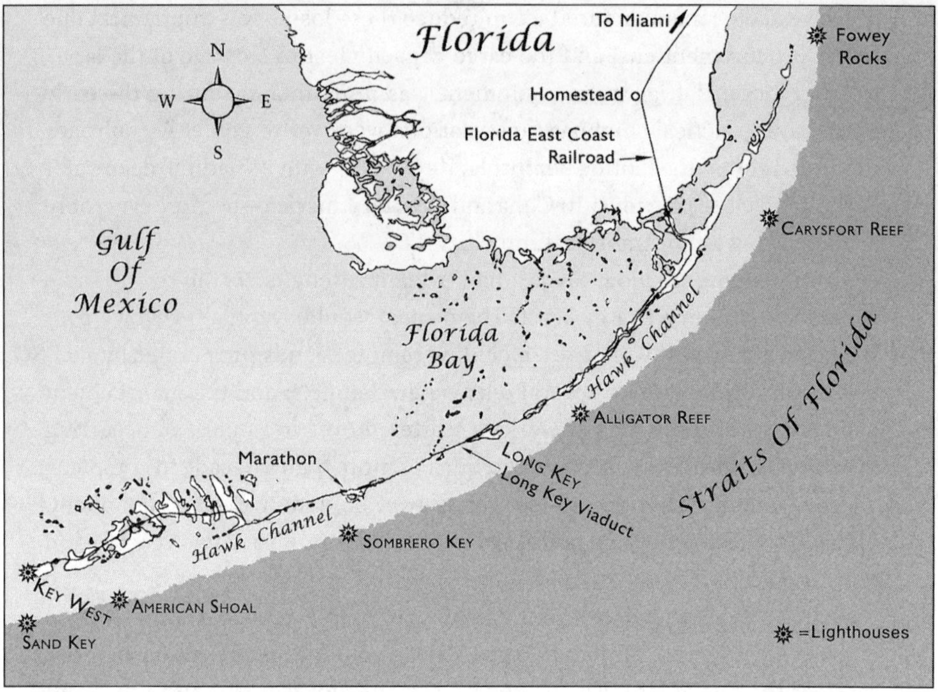

Route of the Florida East Coast Railway from Homestead to Key West. The extension of the railroad from Homestead to Key West involved crossing twenty-nine islands and bridging or filling forty-three waterways. Tidal forces moved enormous amounts of water between the Gulf of Mexico and the Florida Straits, creating strong currents in many of the water openings. This was particularly true of the opening crossed by the Long Key Viaduct. Map by Thomas Neil Knowles.

Long Key contained about 1,000 acres of dry land. Most of it was on the east part of the island, the snake's jaws that partially enclosed a shallow lagoon and mud flat, a place sheltered from the sea breeze and rendered inhospitable by oppressive heat, humidity, and mosquitoes. Florida Bay and the Everglades lie off its north shore, while the south shore faces Hawk Channel, the reef along the Florida Straits, and the Atlantic Ocean.

The Florida Bay shoreline was reported by early surveyors to be composed of ragged coral rock. Inland a spine of higher ground led to an elongated plain that ran from the hinge of the jaw down to the west end of the island. The ocean shoreline was for the most part a continuous white-sand beach. At the east end the beach transitioned inland to a mangrove-filled marsh lining the lagoon. Toward the west end, the beach was fringed by several hundred acres of flat land sprinkled with a few palmettos. In 1858 a surveyor reported that between the end of the island and its neighbors to the west, "a channel leads across the reef into the bay. It can be used by vessels drawing not more than seven feet."[3]

Even though there was no freshwater source other than rain, the plain and the access provided by the channel attracted two commercial ventures to the west end of the island during the nineteenth century. The first was led by Henry Perrine, a medical doctor who became an entrepreneurial botanist while serving as U.S. consul in Campeche, Mexico. Perrine and two partners formed the Tropical Plant Company with the intention of developing agriculturally based industries in south Florida, which at that time was a wild and sparsely settled territory. In 1838 Perrine moved his family to Indian Key, a small island community of about fifty people 8 miles northeast of Long Key, to begin test plantings and other experiments in the Florida Keys. There he successfully bred silkworms and demonstrated that the environment was viable for the production of raw silk.[4]

Perrine fed his worms with mulberry leaves imported from New York during this experimental phase. A local source of mulberry leaves was needed to feed the large number of worms required to produce silk on a commercial scale. In mid-July 1840, he wrote to a New York associate and proposed that mulberry be planted on the prairie at Long Key that autumn. Unfortunately, the Second Seminole Indian War was in progress, and Perrine was killed three weeks later when a war party from the Everglades attacked Indian Key. The plans for a silk industry in the Florida Keys died with him.[5]

In 1879 the prairie was bought by two brothers, Thomas and Edward Hine, and another man, Samuel Filer, for a coconut plantation that would produce copra and coconut-husk fiber. The fiber was in demand by marine cordage manufacturers because it increased the tensile strength of anchor rope. During the next decade, thousands of coconut trees were planted on Long Key. In 1894 *Scribner's Magazine* reported: "There is a grove of cocoa-nuts, numbering over seventeen thousand trees on Long Key, planted by Mr. Thomas Hine, of Newark, N.J., many of which have already come into bearing." When the railroad right-of-way surveyors came along a decade later the area was covered with mature, graceful palm trees.[6]

The route ran across Long Key over the spine of higher ground. The right-of-way began at the northeast tip of the island as a 400-foot-wide swath running down the upper jaw for 1¼ miles, where it changed to a 100-foot-wide corridor that continued to the west end of the key. At that point the right-of-way widened to 400 feet and continued over the water to the westward islands.[7]

In addition to the right-of-way, Flagler acquired the westernmost 45 acres

Thousands of palm trees were removed from the west end of Long Key to clear the right-of-way for the railroad and to make space for the work camp. Courtesy of the Wright Langley Archives.

of Long Key that contained most if not all of the former coconut plantation. The property spanned the island from the white-sand beach on the ocean side to the rocky shore along the bay. The railroad right-of-way came through it, resulting in about a fourth of the acreage being on the ocean side and the remainder on the bay side. Some of the large site was used for a staging area and work camp to support the construction of a crossing from Long Key to Grassy Key to the west.[8]

Except for Conch Key, a small island near the midpoint, the 5.8-mile crossing had to be built over water. The 2.8-mile water opening between Long Key and Conch Key was relatively deep and served as a major conduit for tidal flows between the Gulf of Mexico and the Atlantic Ocean. The railroad's engineers decided to use a concrete viaduct rather than a trestle for most of this part of the crossing because of the forces exerted by strong tides. The railroad viaduct is a very strong structure similar in construction to a Roman viaduct except that the trough that carried water in the Roman version was used to hold the roadbed and track. From Conch Key to Grassy Key, the water would be spanned initially by wooden trestles.

The Long Key Viaduct was constructed by pouring hollow arches on concrete piers anchored to piles driven into bedrock. The voids above the arches were filled and compacted to form the roadbed. Courtesy of the Monroe County Public Library.

The viaduct was originally connected to the west end of Long Key by a trestle built on a fill. The trestle was then buried by the placement of additional fill material. The elevation of the top of the rails on the approach rose from 11 feet above mean sea level at the island end to 21 feet above mean sea level at the viaduct end. The track visible in this circa 1907 photograph was installed to facilitate the movement of fill and was removed after construction was completed. Courtesy of the Monroe County Public Library.

In August 1906, hundreds of workers began to build the approaches, 180 massive concrete arches that comprised the viaduct, and more than 1,500 feet of wooden trestle that crossed the shallow water. The Long Key work camp grew from a few tents to a large facility consisting of warehouses, housing, a central kitchen, hospital, library, and marina. The marina was built on the bay side and included a substantial pier with fueling station, machine shops, and a marine railway for servicing the fleet of vessels supporting the work.[9]

By the middle of October 1906, a large workforce and an impressive fleet of boats, dredges, and barges were at work building the viaduct, trestle, and approaches. Most of the workers lived aboard floating dormitories known as quarter boats, which could be moved as construction progressed. The larger of these vessels were 130' × 30' barges with a wood-framed, two-story building on the upper deck that contained stacked bunks. The space within the wood-planked hull housed a kitchen, dining room, and other support facilities. Quarter boats could accommodate 150 to 175 men and were typically moored to clusters of piling driven into the sea bottom at a location convenient to the worksite.[10]

On October 17, 1906, a hurricane crossed over Cuba, passing east of Havana and into the Florida Straits. With maximum winds at slightly over 120 mph, the hurricane accelerated toward the northeast. Work at the Long Key site was on an around-the-clock schedule, but by midnight the wind had become so strong that the men were sent back to their quarters.[11]

Many of the workers on the viaduct project were housed in floating dormitories called "quarter boats." In this circa 1907 photograph, two quarter boats are shown moored to the dock at the marina on the bay side of the west end of Long Key. Courtesy of the Wright Langley Archives.

A quarter boat was basically a wood-frame building mounted on a large barge. Freshwater was obtained from large cypress water tanks mounted on another barge. In this photograph, the tanks can be seen to the right of the quarter boat. Courtesy of the Wright Langley Archives.

At 7:30 the next morning, winds estimated at 100 mph were blowing from the north with such force that the mooring cables securing quarter boat No. 4 parted. The vessel was quickly swept south into Hawk Channel and carried over the reef into the Florida Straits. After an hour and a half in rough seas, the dormitory atop the barge washed overboard and the hull began to come apart. Floating wreckage from the quarter boat and other craft blown out to sea spread across the shipping lanes of the Florida Straits during the afternoon. Fortunate survivors were picked up by merchant ships, but death claimed one hundred Long Key Viaduct workers and another twenty-seven railroad people who were aboard a Florida East Coast paddle-wheel steamer sunk by the storm in Biscayne Bay off Elliott Key. The dramatic destruction of the quarter boat became part of the hurricane lore of the Florida Keys. Newcomers were certain to hear a telling of it by old-timers, often embellished for maximum effect.[12]

After the "Quarter Boat Hurricane," the Florida East Coast Railway management was much more appreciative of the need for vigilance when it came to monitoring weather conditions during hurricane season as well as the need to avoid the overuse of fills that could block the flow of storm-driven water

On January 22, 1908, the first train to cross the Long Key Viaduct pulled a boxcar and Henry Flagler's two private cars with Flagler, his railroad executives, and some guests onboard. Flagler and his entourage were en route to Knights Key, about 20 miles west of Long Key, where a temporary Florida East Coast steamship/railroad terminal was about to open. Regular passenger service commenced on the viaduct and the line to Knights Key on February 8, 1908. The terminal was abandoned four years later, when the 45 miles of track between Knights Key and Key West were completed. Courtesy of the Wright Langley Archives.

or wooden trestles that could not withstand such flows. Before the Key West Extension was opened in 1912, the wooden trestles of the Long Key crossing were replaced by forty-two additional concrete arches, and the Long Key Viaduct increased its total length to 2.15 miles.[13]

Compared to steel box trestles such as the ones used to cross the Bahia Honda channel to the west, the Long Key Viaduct had no structure above the roadbed and had a low profile when viewed from the side. People standing on the upper decks of large ships sailing just over the horizon in the Florida Straits were treated to a strange optical illusion. One observer wrote: "The trains running along the top present a weird spectacle when viewed from the deck of a vessel. While still miles out at sea the trains running over the top of this viaduct are plainly discernible from steamers. The viaduct, however, owing to the convex surface of the earth, cannot be seen from a distance and the trains appear to be sailing through the air when first they come into view." It was not long before the Key West Extension became known as the Oversea Railroad.[14]

The arches of the Long Key Viaduct seem to stretch to the horizon in this photograph taken in 1926. Heavy locomotives typically used in mountainous terrain ran the Key West Extension to reduce the possibility of the train being blown off the narrow viaducts. The Florida East Coast Railway had a rule that forbade the operation of trains over bridges when the wind exceeded 50 mph. Wind gauges installed on the Long Key Viaduct automatically actuated signals and cross arms to prevent an approaching train from proceeding onto the viaduct when the wind was above the prescribed limit. Courtesy of the State Archives of Florida, *Florida Memory*, http://floridamemory.com.

3

From Work Camp to Fishing Camp

> At the northern end of Long Key, two great viaducts span the sea; between them a long limestone fill [Craig]. The most southerly span is known as Channel #5; the other, Channel #2. They derived their names from the passes which cut through the keys at those points during the construction of the Overseas Railroad. Channels #3 and #4 disappeared when the limestone fill came along, and the water which formerly ebbed and flowed through them became concentrated in the other two, with the consequence that the tide through these channels is terribly swift and strong, a speed of fifteen and eighteen miles an hour being attained at some points. Naturally great quantities of small bait and particles of food are swept off the banks and through these channels; and around the arches of the viaducts, waiting for them, lie the big game fishes, tarpon mostly. . . . By trolling from a very small launch, or light skiff with outboard motor attached, after hooking a fish, should he decide to go through from the Gulf to the Atlantic, or vice versa, cut off your engine, unship your oars, and go through with him.
>
> —Van Campen Heilner, *Adventures in Angling*

Flagler's corporate organization was structured on multiple companies that were highly interactive and, under his firm control, behaved as a unified business entity. The primary ones were registered with the Florida secretary of state between 1895 and 1898. Railroad operations were under the Florida East

Coast Railway Company. Several companies managed real estate acquisitions and sales for the Flagler system, with the Model Land Company being the principal one. The Florida East Coast Steamship Company managed lines to Nassau, Havana, and Key West. The management of the Flagler resorts was the responsibility of the Florida East Coast Hotel Company.[1]

By 1904, when detailed planning for the Key West Extension began, the Florida East Coast Hotel Company had eight magnificent hotels from St. Augustine to Miami and two in the Bahamas, with a combined capacity of five thousand guests. The company had leased a hotel in Key West in 1896 to provide accommodations for passengers brought in by the Florida East Coast Steamship Company. Previously known as the Russell House, it was renovated and opened in February 1897 as the Hotel Key West. The rambling, three-story wood structure located in the commercial district near the steamship docks did have a large bar and a restaurant on the first floor, but it lacked the elegance that had become the trademark of Flagler hotels and offered no resort amenities; there were no grounds and the beach was on the other side of town. The lease was discontinued soon after July 1900, when the Florida East Coast Steamship Company was merged with the Plant Steamship service to form the Peninsular and Occidental Steamship Company. When construction of the railroad to Key West was announced, many of the town's citizens anticipated that another magnificent Flagler resort would be coming to the Island City.[2]

The planning process for the Key West Extension was thorough even to the point of developing a highly detailed clay model of all the islands the railroad would touch and a master plan that showed the Flagler system's vision for Key West. There would be significant physical changes made to the nation's southernmost city. On the north side of the island, the master plan showed a sprawling terminal with a train station, switchyard, and docks for steamers and a railroad ferry, all to be accommodated on a huge tract of new land made from fill dredged to create an expansive deepwater marine facility.

The planners laid out the roadbed to bring the mainline into the terminal facility so that a fill ran across the mouth of a small bay known as Garrison Bight. With a drawbridge installed in the middle of the fill, the bay became a protected harbor for yachts and small craft with waterfront homesites laid out around the yacht basin. At the northeast corner of the island, a spacious site straddling the right-of-way was labeled "Aviation Grounds," an acknowledgment by the Florida East Coast planners of the rapid advancements being made in powered flight. Finally, on the island's south shore, 33 acres of a saltwater marsh were designated as the site for an auditorium.[3]

There were high expectations, some said promises, that Flagler would build another superlative resort at Key West, but the master plan did not identify a site for such a facility. The most likely explanation for this omission is that premature disclosure of the desired location for a hotel would drive the price of the land up. A resort would be built, but it would not become a reality until eight years after Flagler rode the first train into Key West.

In the meantime, the Florida East Coast Hotel Company was interested in the development opportunity afforded by the Long Key construction camp site. The broad sand beach bordered by graceful palms and the clear, multi-hued waters teeming with bonefish, barracuda, tarpon, and numerous other varieties of marine life would impress any visitor. Only 7 miles off the beach lay the deep, blue waters of the Florida Straits and the migratory routes of large game fish. On the north side of the site, Florida Bay provided a sheltered waterway that could be navigated by canoe or small boat to nearby mangrove-shrouded islands that were pristine sanctuaries for birds and other wildlife. Long Key had all the natural ingredients to make an ideal retreat.

That Flagler's alert staff picked up on these features and planned a destination for this location is not surprising; that they would make a radical departure from nineteen years of building imposing hotels surrounded by manicured grounds is a credit to their marketing acumen and their appreciation of the natural environment. They were fortunate to have in their organization a man descended from a long line of hoteliers who specialized in the operation and management of resorts where the main attraction was their natural surroundings.[4]

Louis "L. P." Schutt (pronounced "Skutt" to rhyme with "gut") was born about 1863 in Greene County, New York, a region of incredible beauty in the Catskill Mountains. A descendant of European innkeepers, his grandfather built the first hotel in the Catskill Mountains in the early 1800s. L. P.'s father, J. Lewis Schutt, carried on the profession and apprenticed his son in the trade. In 1890, after graduating from Miami University (Ohio) and serving as deputy county clerk of Greene County, L. P. leased the Antlers Hotel in Haines Falls, New York, which he operated during the summer and fall seasons. Near the end of the century, he began working for Flagler's Florida East Coast Hotel Company during the winter and spring seasons at their hotels in Nassau.

He was dispatched in 1906 by the Flagler corporate management to the Florida Keys, or, as the *New York Times* phrased it, he was "induced to leave Nassau and take charge of feeding for two years of as many as 4,500 men" who were building the railroad to Key West. This may have been his original assignment, but not long after his arrival, the idea of creating a rustic fishing

When this photograph was taken in 1906, only temporary construction track was laid on the Long Key roadbed. The buildings in the background would become the core structures of the fishing camp. Courtesy of the State Archives of Florida, *Florida Memory*, http://floridamemory.com.

resort had gained traction at the corporate headquarters, and a year later L. P. Schutt was named manager of the Long Key Fishing Camp.[5]

At that time the fishing camp consisted of a few buildings that had housed senior managers and technical staff during construction. A report believed to have been prepared by L. P. Schutt soon after his appointment as manager advised H. E. Bemis, who was coordinating the fishing-camp project for the Florida East Coast Hotel Company, that certain improvements were needed to convert the former work-camp facilities into a complex that would "impress anyone as a good attraction and substantial proposition."[6]

For example, while building the approach to the viaduct, draglines had scooped up quantities of material from the beach, leaving a narrow strand of the original shoreline between the excavation and the water. This borrow pit became a substantial pond of trapped rainwater. The report stated: "It is impossible to have any kind of camp until this beach is filled. It is a bad breeding place for mosquitoes and as the prevailing winds are from the ocean, the smell at night is bad."

The report called for the construction of a large building that would invite social interaction and provide a place for guests to go on blustery days when wintry winds kept the fishing boats tied up. "There should be one good building, well built with good porches, 2 stories high, 48 ft square to be buolt [*sic*] substantially having shingled sides and ceiled [*sic*] all through. First floor to contain office and large sitting space public toilet and bath rooms for men and women. The second floor to have large sitting and writing rooms on front and six double sleeping rooms. It is important to have one good cheerful building of this kind with large porches where everyone can meet in stormy weather, keep warm and kill time. There are days when there is no fishing—this will be needed and also for care of transient business." This building, known as the lodge, became the iconic structure of the Long Key Fishing Camp.

As recommended in the report, two construction camp buildings were combined to create a food-service facility. Bunk House No. 4, a wood-frame structure 90 feet long and 23 feet wide, was selected for the dining room and was relocated near the train station and attached to an existing smaller building that was to serve as the kitchen/icehouse/pantry facility. The unattached end of the dining room faced the beach and was adjacent to the northwest corner of the lodge. A breezeway connected the lodge to a covered, broad porch constructed to dress up the drab end of the former bunkhouse. The dining room had a splendid view of the beach from the porch, while the windows on its west side commanded a full view of the viaduct.

The locations of the lodge and food-service facilities were given considerable thought. Grouping them together provided convenient access to food and drinks for guests attending social events at the lodge. Also, the lodge, dining room, and kitchen were sited such that they could be enlarged in the future with minimum impact on other buildings of the fishing camp. Placing the cold storage locker and pantry near the train station enabled food, ice, and other supplies to be delivered via a chute direct from the baggage platform.

The dining room and lodge established the focal point for social and business activity at the camp. In accordance with recommendations in the report, a complex of bungalows for guests was created in the palm grove east of the lodge by converting buildings that had previously served as housing for viaduct construction personnel. The small houses that had been the quarters of senior personnel and technical staff were renovated into two-guest and four-guest bungalows.

Near the edge of the palm grove, between the small bungalows and the beach, four bunkhouses, 60 feet long by 23 feet wide, were relocated and placed so that their narrow ends faced the beach. Each was renovated to hold eight guests by dividing it in half with a full-length partition and then partitioned again to create four, single-guest rooms on each side. Each room had a door opening onto a side veranda and another door in its opposite wall that could be unlocked to access the adjoining room, thereby making a two-room suite.

The plan laid out in the report produced a resort that could comfortably house seventy guests in five two-guest bungalows, four four-guest bungalows, four eight-guest bungalows, and six two-guest rooms in the lodge. The arrangement was unlike that of any other resort in the Florida East Coast Hotel Company.

A newspaper reported in October 1908 that six buildings were being erected at Long Key "to allow the traveling public to enjoy some of the best fishing in the world." Another newspaper noted that L. P. Schutt, manager of the Long Key Fishing Camp, had been appointed postmaster of the Long Key Post Office on December 28, 1908.[7]

The January 20, 1909, edition of the *Florida Star* announced that Long Key had changed from a work camp to a tourist destination.

> Long Key has undergone a complete transformation. It is now headquarters for the tourists who come down to see the extension work although there are quite a few at the "hotel boat" at Knights Key.
>
> There are still quite a number of men at work at Long Key, but the improvements there are nearing completion and the entire force will shortly be moved southward.[8]

The *Daytona Gazette-News* on July 17, 1909, stated that the Long Key Fishing Camp season for 1909–10 would be from Wednesday, December 1, 1909, until Monday, April 18, 1910. Less than three weeks later, the *Key West Citizen* proclaimed Long Key "one of the most attractive places along the line," noting that the facilities now included "a two-story hotel" and thirty bungalows.[9]

A brochure for the 1909–10 season listing hotels at locations served by the Florida East Coast Railway carried this description of the fishing camp:

> The buildings are located in a beautiful grove of cocoanut palms on the southeastern extremity of the island, overlooking a charming bay with gently shelving hard sand beach. . . . The camp consists of a number of small cottages with a central building as office, reading room, etc., the kitchen and dining room being in a separate building.
>
> Too much cannot be said in praise of the beauty of the camp and surroundings. To the eastward, a short mile, flows that mysterious river in the ocean—the Gulf Stream. Large vessels, steam and sail, moving southward

> are almost constantly in sight, sailing close to the Keys to avoid the current of the Gulf Stream, and laving the shore of the Key on the west is the Gulf of Mexico.

The announcement stated that the camp could house and feed one hundred guests and that lodging with three meals daily cost $3.00 (approximately equivalent to $78.10 in 2012) and up. The fare for the 457-mile trip from Jacksonville to Long Key was $14.45 ($376.00 in 2012) each way.

There were concerns that the unpretentiousness of the fishing camp could come as a shock to some of the clientele accustomed to the elegant buildings, white-glove service, and groomed lawns of other resorts of the Florida East Coast Hotel Company. This prompted the inclusion of the following unusually frank cautionary notice.

> Prospective patrons should not get the idea that this camp is luxurious in its appointment and that the table and service will be maintained on a par with the hotels of the Florida East Coast Hotel Company. It is, rather, a typical subtropical "fishing camp" with everything complete, sanitary and comfortable, located in the center of the famous fishing grounds of the Floridian archipelago. The table will be abundantly supplied with sea food, fruits and vegetables properly prepared and satisfactorily served.[10]

That the Long Key Fishing Camp was considered the homely stepchild of the Flagler hotels was signaled when the fishing camp was conspicuously left out of a two-page spread featuring Florida East Coast Hotel Company resorts that appeared in a 1912 brochure published by the railroad to formally announce the opening of the Key West Extension. Even in black-and-white, the images of the Ponce de Leon, Alcazar, and Cordova hotels in St. Augustine, the Ormond in Ormond-on-the-Halifax, the Royal Poinciana and the Breakers in Palm Beach, the Royal Palm in Miami, and the Colonial in Nassau radiated magnificence and luxury. [11]

This corporate slight did not bother L. P. Schutt; the management and promotion of resorts that emphasized their natural setting rather than spectacular edifices was a family tradition. Ironically, it occurred just as the fishing camp was about to become known worldwide. Advertisements for the Long Key Fishing Camp often mentioned that it was managed by L. P. Schutt, which drew some of the people who had previously experienced his hospitality at resorts in the Catskills and Bahamas. Even so, the camp remained relatively unknown until it was discovered by a lanky dentist from the Midwest who preferred writing novels and fishing to installing fillings.

L. P. Schutt (*right*), manager of the Long Key Fishing Camp, chats with two men believed to be William J. Krome and L. C. Haines at the Long Key train station in 1910. Krome became chief engineer of the Key West Extension project in 1909, and Haines became treasurer of the Florida East Coast Railway in 1914. Courtesy of the State Archives of Florida, *Florida Memory*, http://floridamemory.com.

His western *The Heritage of the Desert* became an instant best seller in 1910, and the thirty-eight-year-old author decided to celebrate with a trip to Tampico for some tarpon fishing with his brother. They were en route aboard a Ward liner when the captain informed them that the ship would not be stopping at the Mexican port because of an outbreak of yellow fever. The men disembarked at Nassau and, as the author put it, "accidentally dropped into Long Key." Not only did Zane Grey catch some fine fish, but he was hooked and returned regularly to Long Key thereafter.[12]

Grey's *Riders of the Purple Sage* appeared in bookstores two years later; it would become the most popular western novel ever published, selling well over 1 million copies. As his prominence as an author grew, so did the publicity of the excellent fishing he enjoyed at Long Key. His fans ranged from royalty to blue-collar workers, from students to octogenarians. Grey's activities were closely followed by the media and his visits to the Long Key Fishing Camp were often reported in magazines and newspapers. Long Key rapidly became known worldwide for outstanding sportfishing, a reputation maintained throughout its existence because of the camp's facilities, location, fishing club, and consistent management.[13]

Zane Grey (*left*) and his brother Romer pose with their catch at Long Key in 1916. Zane Grey was a dentist turned best-selling author, and was primarily responsible for Long Key becoming known worldwide for its outstanding sportfishing. An avid fisherman, he was a founding member of the Long Key Fishing Club and a regular guest at the camp for twenty-five years. Courtesy of the State Archives of Florida, *Florida Memory*, http://floridamemory.com.

4

A Fishing Camp Extraordinaire

> In three fathoms of water we could see every detail of the coral formation, with its changing hues and the deep caverns, every one of which probably harbored a big jack. Fish were everywhere—the beautiful speckled cero, swift as light; the long, lean-jawed barracuda, floating in the amber water; the thick-bodied, dark-brown groupers, boldly on a scavenger hunt; the blue and gold jacks, lying far down in the shadow of coral blocks. I think it no exaggeration to say that we could not drag a spoon ten feet along that reef without seeing the water boil with fish. The smaller ones always reached the spoon first and by smaller fish I mean cero or barracuda of five to ten pounds. When we hooked one of these, the big fellows soared up and there was a heavy splash, bloody foam, and only enough bait left for a not too particular grouper.
>
> —Zane Grey, "The Amberjack of Sombrero Reef"

The Long Key Fishing Camp could provide lodging, board, boats, guides, bait, and tackle as needed. Fuel, ice, and potable water were available for visiting yachts, these items being brought in regularly by the railroad from the mainland. Anything needed that was not readily available at the camp could be delivered by train in a matter of a day or two.

The single-track Florida East Coast Railway mainline divided the property into two distinct areas: the bay side containing approximately 34 acres and the ocean side comprising about 11 acres. The most imposing structures on the

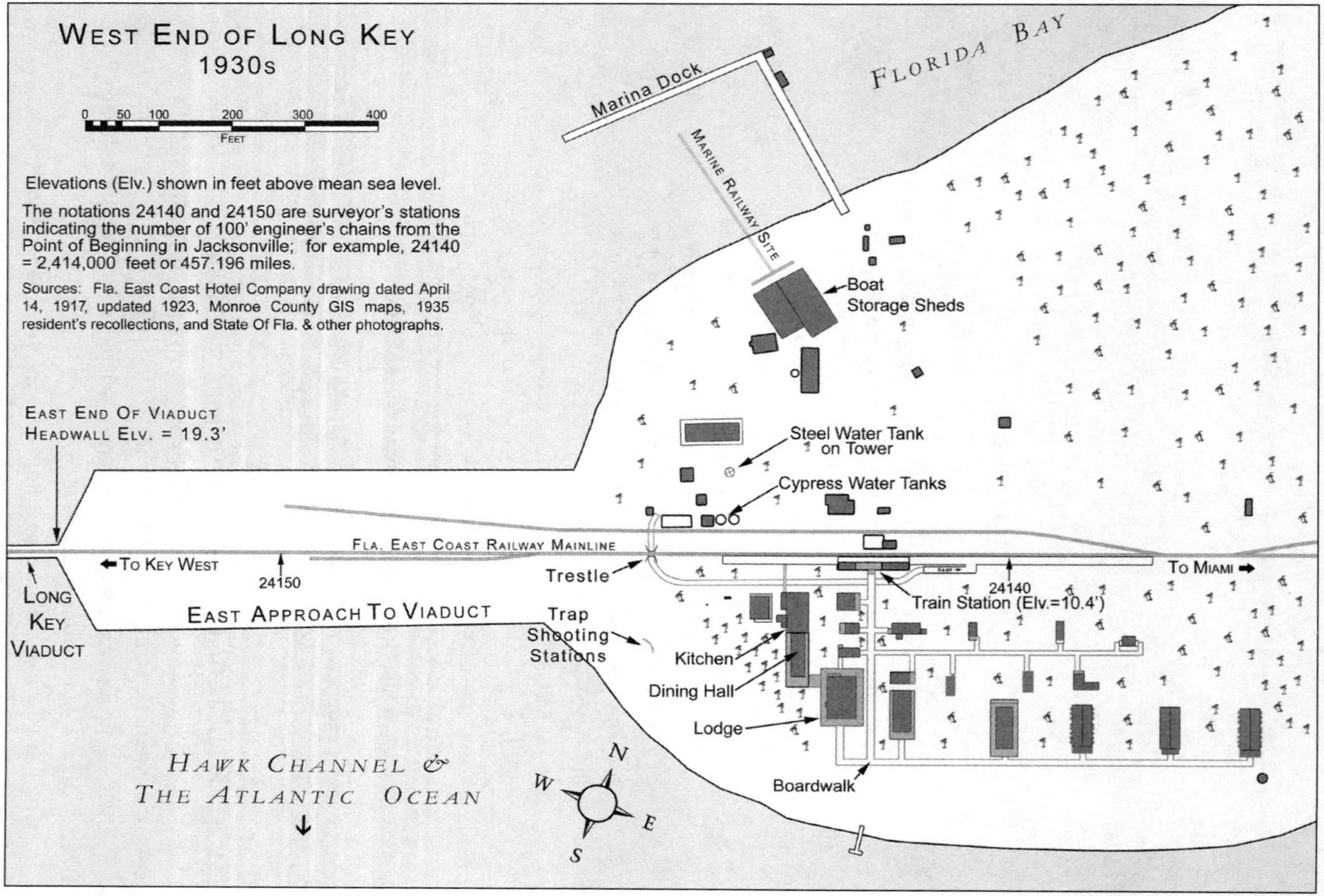

The west end of Long Key, 1930s. The Florida East Coast Railway mainline divided the Long Key Fishing Camp site into the "bay side" and the "ocean side." Map by Thomas Neil Knowles.

bay side were two large shed-like buildings sitting side by side and the dock. The sheds were linked to a marine railway that had been used in servicing the fleet of vessels deployed to construct the viaduct. Now the sheds were used to service the resort's own fleet, which included marine craft from canoes to cabin cruisers, and to store them during the off-season.

A doglegged dock almost as long as two football fields wrapped around the marine railway to form a sheltered lagoon. The pier ran from the shore 250 feet into the water where the dockmaster's office and bait house were located; it then turned 90 degrees and ran 300 feet parallel to the shore toward the Long Key Viaduct. Catches could be registered for recognition by international fishing organizations at the official weigh station next to the dockmaster's office. A taxidermist's shop was conveniently located on the shore near the end of the dock. A large gasoline storage tank onshore supplied fuel for vessels via a gravity-fed pipe to the gasoline pump installed next to the bait house.[1]

In between the marina and the Florida East Coast Railway mainline were facilities for feeding and housing resort workers, a railroad-equipment storage building, carpenter's shop, Coast Guard office, laundry, and a large, elevated steel tank. A siding ran down along the mainline to a utilities area occupied by twin elevated cypress water tanks, a small steam plant/pumping station, and a coal bin.

Just beyond this group of utility facilities was the gas plant, a small building that housed equipment used to produce acetylene gas for interior and exterior lighting and the stove in the central kitchen. The original plan for the camp recommended the use of acetylene because the gas plant could be built for a quarter of the cost of an electric generator plant. At the time many small towns, hotels, and remote estates too small to maintain central electric plants or coal gas plants used acetylene because the fuel (calcium carbide) was fairly cheap and gave a light superior in quality to any common artificial illuminant except for the electric arc lamp.[2]

Perhaps the greatest advantage of acetylene for places like the camp was that the gas generator ran automatically for weeks without the need for an attendant. Even when service was required, it did not have to be performed by a highly skilled workman and did not take much time because the machinery had few moving parts and the only consumables involved were solid fuel cartridges and freshwater. The gas plant was only operational when the camp was open for guests. During the off-season, kerosene lamps provided interior lighting in the caretaker's bungalow and other buildings occupied by maintenance personnel.

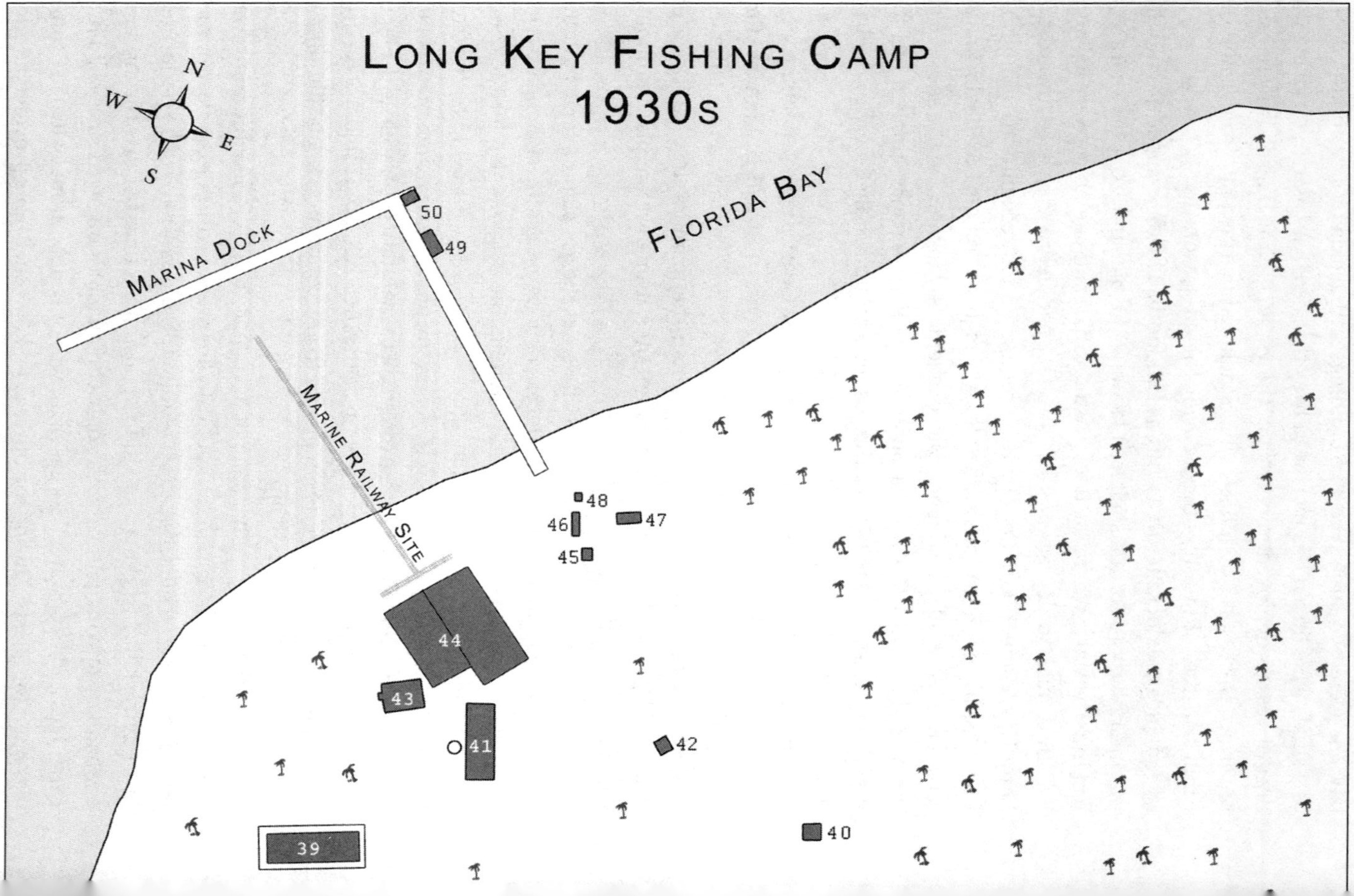

Long Key Fishing Camp
1930s
N
W
E
S
Marina Dock
Florida Bay
Marine Railway Site
50
49
48
47
46
45
44
43
41
42
39
40

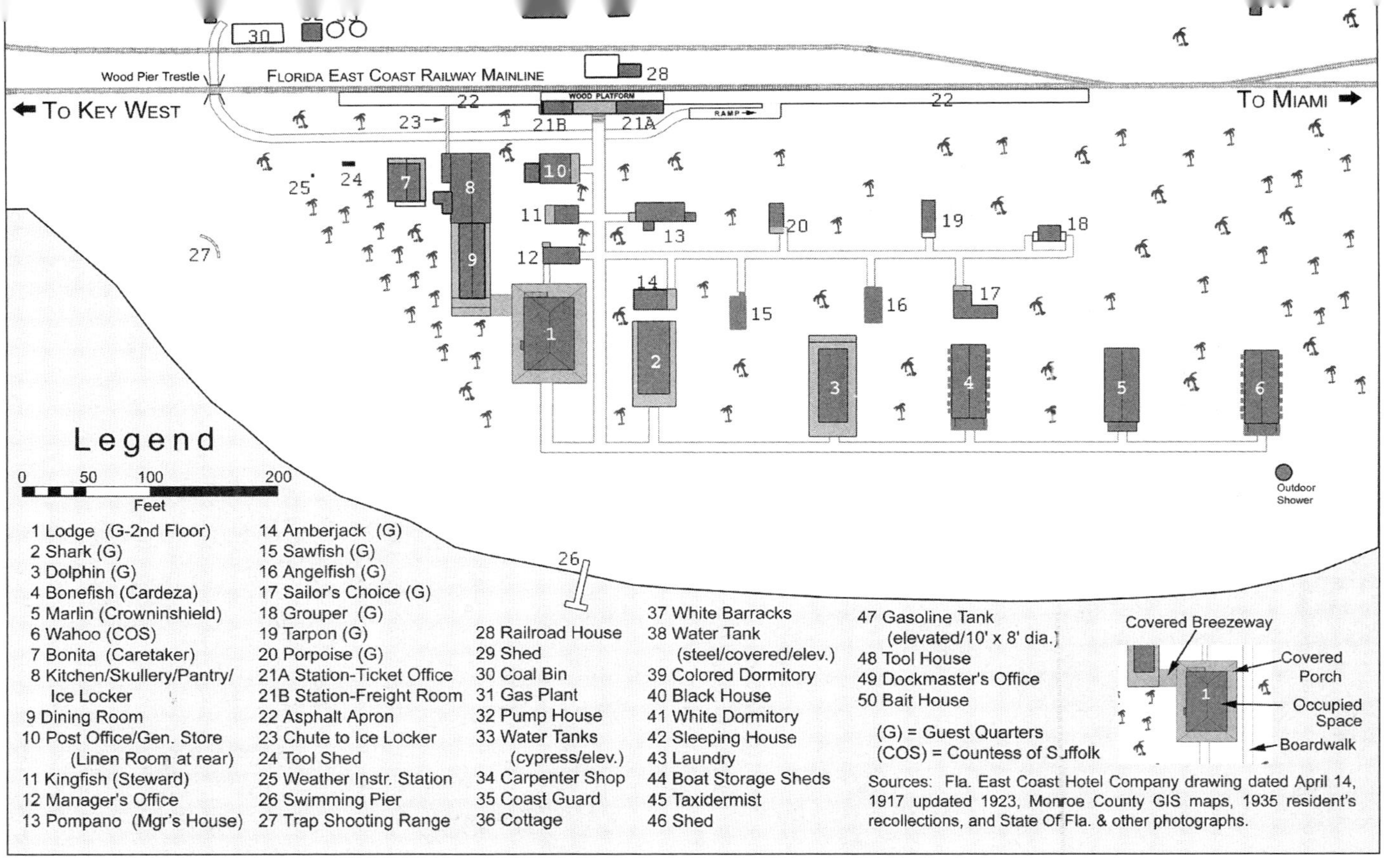

The Long Key Fishing Camp layout, 1930s. Map by Thomas Neil Knowles.

The Long Key Fishing Camp had a fleet of boats available to its guests, ranging from canoes and skiffs for fishing inshore waters (*foreground*) to cabin cruisers that roamed the reef and ventured into the Gulf Stream. Courtesy of the Wright Langley Archives.

From the midpoint of Long Key westward, the Florida East Coast Railway mainline ran along the top of a sloping embankment for 2½ miles that raised the roadbed from near the natural grade up to 20 feet above mean sea level at the east end of the viaduct. In the area of the train station, the embankment was a solid fill about 6 feet above the natural grade. To facilitate the unrestricted movement of materials between the bay side and the ocean side during the construction of the viaduct, a small, wood-pile trestle was installed in the embankment 283 feet west of the station. This created a tunnel just big enough for a narrow-gauge tram to pass through the embankment at ground level. When the viaduct was completed, the tram rails were removed and replaced with a path made of railroad ties to maintain convenient access to both sides of the property.[3]

The tunnel also facilitated the delivery of gas, potable water, salt water, and steam from the utility facilities on the bay side to the buildings on the ocean side of the camp. The piping was run beneath the tunnel's railroad-tie road and then under the boardwalk to the buildings, keeping it out of sight of the guests.

To conserve freshwater, all toilets and showers at the camp operated with salt water. Sewage was collected via underground pipes and discharged at the first arch of the Long Key Viaduct, where tidal currents carried it out to sea.

The Long Key train station was originally located on the bay side of the track. In addition to being too small, the building was located on the wrong side of the tracks for detraining fishing-camp guests. It was replaced in 1920 by a more spacious station on the ocean side with broad steps leading directly down to the boardwalk that threaded its way among the camp's buildings so the guests could walk from one place to another without getting sand in their shoes.

The largest building on the ocean side was the two-story lodge. With double-decked, 12-foot-wide verandas on all four sides, a tall brick chimney, and a roof-mounted flagpole flying a large American flag, the lodge stood majestic and serene, only a stone's throw across the beach from the water. Most of the first floor was occupied by the front desk/office and a spacious lounge dominated by a large fireplace. The walls and supporting columns were crowded with mounted trophies of fish, birds, and deer taken by guests. The second floor was devoted to guest rooms, a writing room, and a sitting room. The south and west sides faced the beach that curved around the building. On the east side, fourteen guest cabins nestled among the palms.

A covered breezeway connected the northwest corner of the lodge to the porch of the dining room. The kitchen, icehouse, manager's office, and general store/post office occupied the intervening space to the mainline. Ice manufactured at a plant near Homestead was unloaded from trains by sliding the 300-pound blocks down a chute direct to the icehouse. In the kitchen, a chef assisted by several cooks prepared meals three times a day as well as box lunches for guests going fishing or on other day trips. Everything was prepared on-site including cookies and candy. The post office and general store shared a square-shaped structure topped with a small clerestory.

The cabins occupied by guests and some of the staff were referred to as bungalows and were identified by the names of fish rather than numbers. Some of the small guest bungalows were plain buildings with vertically run slat siding and galvanized metal roofs. They had roofless wood decks for a porch served by plain wood steps. Bungalows reserved for the exclusive use of certain patrons had full-width screened porches and were much larger. The building closest to the viaduct on the ocean side was the Bonita, the caretaker's cabin. The easternmost building was the large bungalow built for the Dowager Countess of Suffolk and Berkshire around 1930.

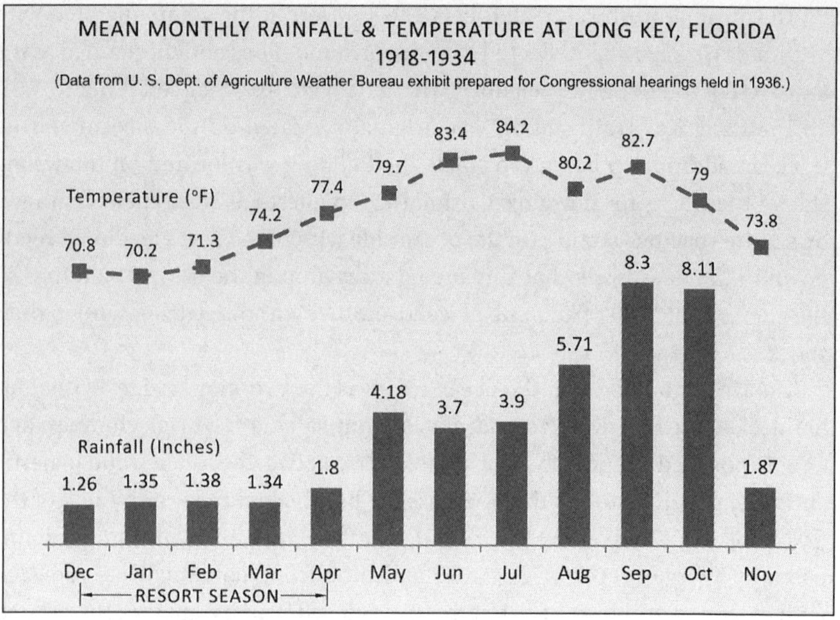

From 1918 through 1934, the annual mean temperature at Long Key was 77.5°F, and the annual cumulative mean rainfall was 42.9 inches. The Long Key Fishing Camp season could begin as early as the middle of December and close as late as the middle of April, which coincided with the island's mildest weather period. Graph by Thomas Neil Knowles.

All buildings were built on piles with the floor raised about 2 feet above the sand that covered the grounds of the resort. Many of the bungalows and some other buildings were painted with "Florida East Coast" yellow, a color that blended nicely with the green, brown, and yellow palms surrounding them.

Freshwater for the fishing camp was delivered by train from the mainland because rainfall was not sufficient to make its collection and storage in cisterns practical during the four months the resort was open. From December to April, rainfall averaged less than 1.5 inches per month at Long Key, and much of that was intercepted by the overhanging palm trees. During the off-season, the average rainfall was more than 5 inches per month.[4]

Provisions at the Long Key Fishing Camp for personal hygiene were basic compared to the other resorts of the Flagler system. Each guest room was provided with a sponge, a pitcher of freshwater, and large bowl as well as a chamber pot. Bathing was typically a two-stage process; first a saltwater shower followed by a freshwater sponge bath to rinse off; a 1920s female guest described the arrangement as similar to camping out.[5]

There were two bathtubs available for the use of guests, one for men and one for women. The tubs were located on the first floor of the lodge in small rooms near the front desk. Each tub was provided with both saltwater and freshwater spigots. A preprinted item for "Baths" on the camp's standard billing form indicates that the tubs were available at an extra charge and probably with a surcharge for freshwater.[6]

Top: Trains made up of flatcars, each carrying two large cypress water tanks, regularly delivered potable water to the Long Key Fishing Camp and most of the Florida East Coast facilities in the Florida Keys. The water came from a well field on the mainland southeast of Homestead. As the train proceeded toward Key West, flatcars were detached so that the water could be pumped into elevated tanks; they were picked up on the return trip. *Bottom*: The Long Key potable water tanks were located on a siding on the bay side of the mainline. Courtesy of the Monroe County Public Library.

The large bungalows reserved for the exclusive use of the Cardezas, Crowninshield, and the Countess of Suffolk respectively most likely were equipped with whatever personal hygiene facilities those patrons were willing to pay for.

There was no outside wiring or other evidence indicating that the camp was served by a central electrical plant; however, it is known that there were devices on the premises in the 1930s that required electricity. For instance, there were broadcast-band radios in the caretaker's cabin and lodge, and electric lamps and fans in the Countess of Suffolk's bungalow. These were probably powered by small, building generators.[7]

The majority of people visiting the resort arrived by train, the camp being 2¾ hours (92 miles) from the Miami train station and 1½ hours (65 miles) from the Key West station. Privately owned vessels, yachts in particular, were the second-most-popular method of reaching the island. Some guests flew from Miami on chartered seaplanes when that service became available after the Great War.

A highway from Miami to Key West was built in the 1920s, but lack of funds left a 40-mile gap. The road from the mainland ended at Lower Matecumbe Key, 6 miles to the east of Long Key, and the highway from Key West terminated 34 miles to the west at No Name Key. Ferries ran between the two ends, but they did not stop at Long Key.[8]

Access to Long Key was primarily by train, but guests also arrived by boat and in later years by chartered seaplane from Miami, as shown in this photograph taken at the fishing camp in 1922. During the camp's existence, civilian passenger aviation evolved and commercial seaplane service became a reality. Courtesy of the Wright Langley Archives.

The first and only automobile to visit the Long Key Fishing Camp arrived in December 1927. A Jacksonville LaSalle dealer staged the publicity stunt by having a car driven down to Key West on the track roadbed. The dealer and driver were closely followed by a motorized flatcar that carried a film crew, mechanic, and spare parts. Crossing the narrow viaducts was the most dangerous part of the journey because the car's rubber-tired wheels had to straddle one of the rails. The bumpy trip was completed without injury or mishap. Courtesy of the Wright Langley Archives.

The isolation of the camp was exploited in later years with ads that highlighted the peace and quiet of the island and the absence of automobiles. The following is an eloquent example:

> Long Key is a beautiful coral island a hundred miles below Miami, with the Gulf of Mexico on one side and the Atlantic on the other. For winter and spring it is one of the most ideal resorts in the United States, having an invigorating yet temperate and frost-free climate and superb connections by rail with New York, Boston, Chicago and the West.
>
> The island is reached by the magnificent overseas extension of the Florida East Coast Railway, with fast direct Pullman service.
>
> It is clean and healthy with the breath of salt air, free from style and pretension, and, with no automobiles, one of the quietest places on earth. By day the wind murmurs its music through the palm trees and by night the sea moans out on the reef. The sun shines white all day and the stars shine white all night. There is a long white winding shoreline of coral sand bordered by palm trees. Long Key has beauty, charm and mystery.[9]

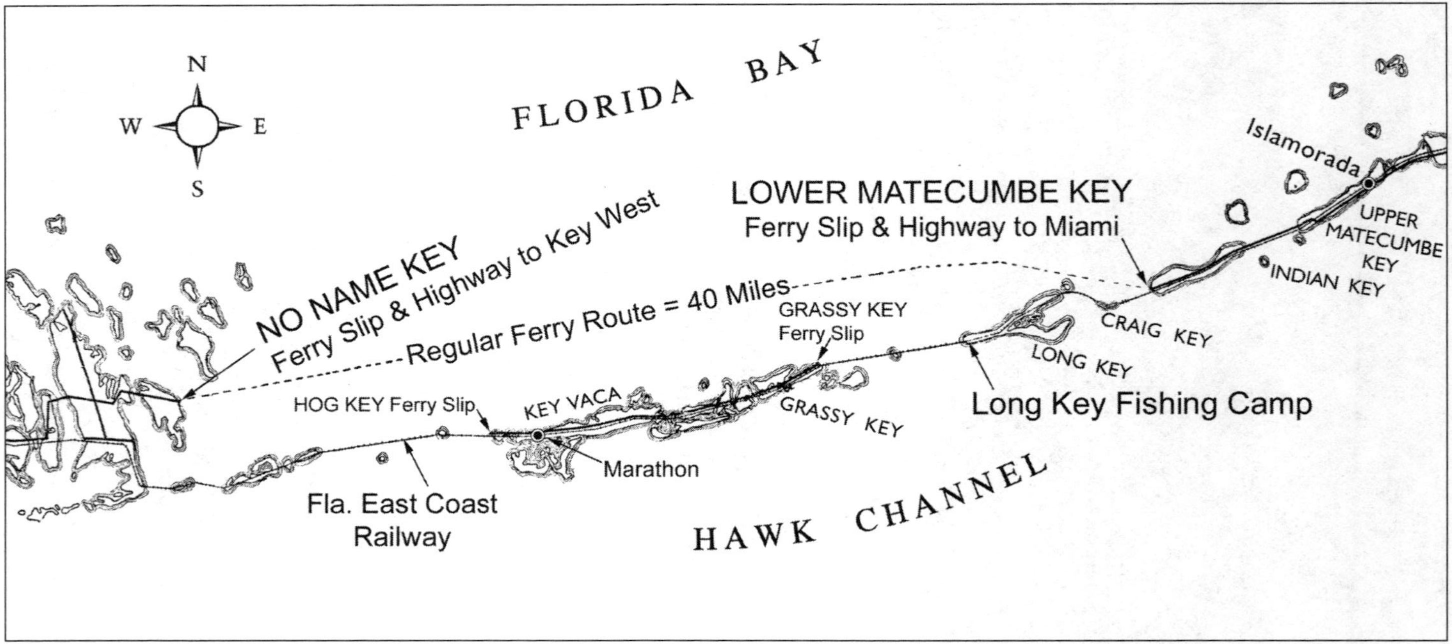

Ferry route between No Name Key and Lower Matecumbe Key. In the late 1920s, the highway down the Florida Keys ran from the mainland to a ferry slip at the west end of Lower Matecumbe Key. Ferries carried vehicles across a 40-mile water gap to No Name Key where the highway to Key West began. The ferries occasionally put into slips at Hog Key and Grassy Key, the ends of a 13-mile strip of road that served the Marathon area. Ferry service was never provided to Long Key. Map by Thomas Neil Knowles.

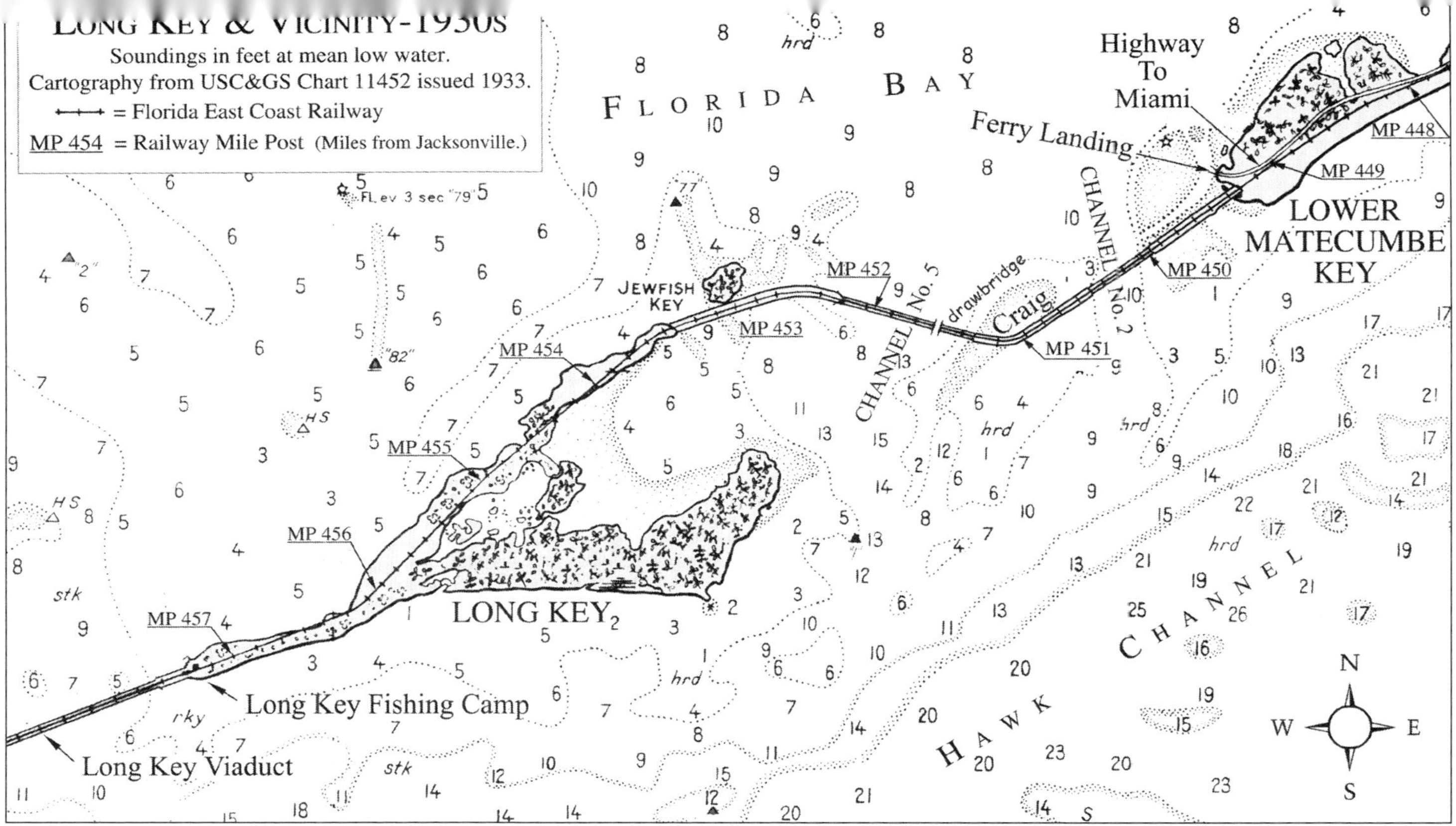

Long Key to Lower Matecumbe Key. The Long Key Viaduct had no drawbridge and a maximum clearance of 25 feet. Vessels with tall masts or superstructures desiring to cross from Florida Bay to Hawk Channel or vice versa used the drawbridge just west of Craig. Map by Thomas Neil Knowles.

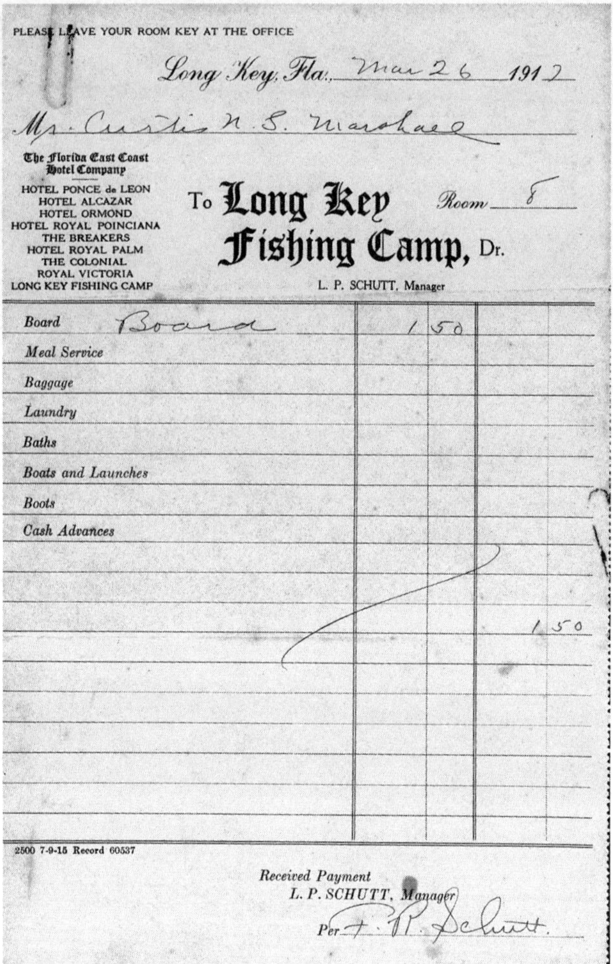

PLEASE LEAVE YOUR ROOM KEY AT THE OFFICE

Long Key, Fla., Mar 26 1912

Mr. Curtis N. S. Marshall

The Florida East Coast Hotel Company

HOTEL PONCE de LEON
HOTEL ALCAZAR
HOTEL ORMOND
HOTEL ROYAL POINCIANA
THE BREAKERS
HOTEL ROYAL PALM
THE COLONIAL
ROYAL VICTORIA
LONG KEY FISHING CAMP

To **Long Key Fishing Camp,** Dr. Room 8

L. P. SCHUTT, Manager

Board Board	1 50		
Meal Service			
Baggage			
Laundry			
Baths			
Boats and Launches			
Boots			
Cash Advances			
			1 50

2500 7-9-15 Record 60537

Received Payment
L. P. SCHUTT, Manager
Per F. R. Schutt.

This copy of a guest's receipt provides an indication of the services available at the camp. The circumstances of a U.S. Marshal's visit to Long Key are not known, but the date on his bill coincides with the retrieval of a wayward naval mine that had washed up on a sandbar and posed a threat to the camp's fishing boats (see chapter 8 for details). Courtesy of the Wright Langley Archives.

There was one telephone at the camp, but it was kept in a locked box in the train station office. Only the stationmaster, the camp manager, and the caretaker had keys to the box. The telephone was restricted to official business use, but the train station had a telegraph, and guests could send and receive messages via that facility as well as through the mail at the post office.[10]

The form used to bill guests for their stay at the Long Key Fishing Camp had seven preprinted items: Board, which included accommodations and meals taken in the dining room; Meal Services, which covered meals for visitors not staying at the camp, box lunches, and room service; Baggage, for handling and storage fees; Laundry; Baths; Boats and Launches, for charter boats and small-boat rental; and Boots, for boot cleaning and shoeshine services. The form also had a line for cash advances and a generous number of blank lines for writing in other charges such as dock fees, fuel, bait, and trap shooting.[11]

The cost of a stay at the Long Key Fishing Camp was not unreasonable, according to the March 1918 issue of *Outing Magazine*: "Board and lodging costs from five to five and a half dollars a day, and boats, including guide services, may be rented for from $15 to $20 per day. Two men taking a bungalow and using the same boat could live very happily on sixteen or seventeen dollars each per diem including tips, smokes, and incidentals."[12]

Some price increases had occurred by 1935; the camp offered rooms in the lodge and in two eight-guest-room buildings at $6.00 to $8.00 daily single occupancy and $10.00 to $15.00 daily for two people. Private bungalows for two to four people were advertised as "usually available" at a charge of $8.00 and $9.00 daily per person. Daily accommodation rates included three meals in the dining room. Even though the Long Key Fishing Camp's rates were considered reasonable, they were more than the average worker could afford, especially when added to the cost to get there.[13]

The expense and limited access served to restrict the regular clientele to the well-to-do. Not all came for the fishing. As a 1921 travel guide noted, a stay at Long Key could have a therapeutic effect. "While the camp is a fisherman's resort, one need not be an angler to enjoy it," wrote Charles Reynolds. "We know of men and women who have gone into retreat on Long Key, and under the spell of its quiet and the soothing charm of the surrounding sea have recovered their poise."[14]

This panoramic 1912 photograph shows the ocean side of the Long Key Fishing Camp. View from west to east showing, *left to right*, the Long Key Viaduct, the East Approach, the lodge, one of the large eight-guest buildings, one of the small bungalows and several additional eight-guest buildings. Courtesy of the Library of Congress.

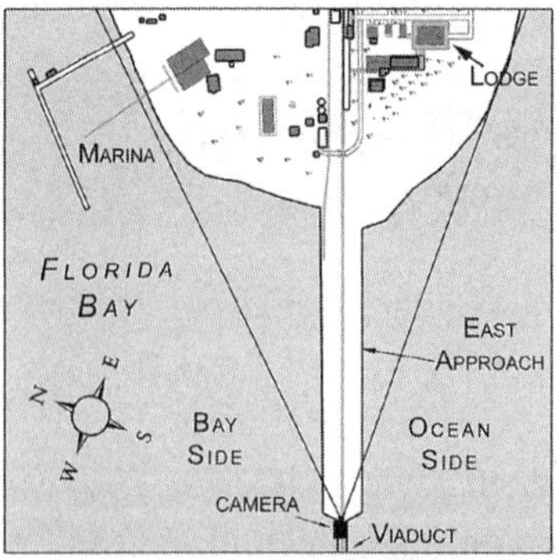

View of the Long Key Fishing Camp from the viaduct. The large building on the ocean side (*right*) is the lodge. The dock at the marina is just off camera on the bay side (*left*). The end of the concrete viaduct was connected to Long Key by a 600-foot fill known as the East Approach. This image was made around 1918, when the seawall on the ocean side of the approach was used as a dock. Courtesy of the Monroe County Public Library.

East of the camp, the beach transitioned into its natural state. At the extreme left, the railing of the train platform can be seen through the coconut trees. Courtesy of the Library of Congress.

A close-up view of the East Approach dock and boardwalk, circa 1918. The lodge, on the right with flag, was the landmark structure of the fishing camp. Courtesy of the Monroe County Public Library.

Around 1920, additional fill was added to the East Approach to make room for a siding adjacent to the mainline. When maintenance was needed on the viaduct or its approaches, several railroad cars were brought in and parked on the siding (*right*). The cars provided living quarters for the workers and storage for their supplies and tools. The ocean-side seawall of the approach was used to pick up guests going out on the camp's cabin cruisers. Circa 1933. Courtesy of Patricia J. Duane.

In 1920, a new train station with a spacious, covered passenger waiting area in the middle was built at Long Key. Courtesy of Patricia J. Duane.

View of the west end of the train station where the baggage room was located. The station was built on piles so that it was at the same elevation as the track, almost 10½ feet above mean sea level. Courtesy of the State Archives of Florida, *Florida Memory*, http://floridamemory.com.

The stationmaster's office was located at the east end of the station. Courtesy of the State Archives of Florida, *Florida Memory*, http://floridamemory.com.

The post office was the first camp building encountered by guests as they left the train station. Readily identifiable by its distinctive cupola, it also housed a small general store where newspapers and sundries were sold. The building behind the post office is part of the kitchen/icehouse complex. Just beyond it, the porch of the caretaker's house is visible. Courtesy of the State Archives of Florida, *Florida Memory*, http://floridamemory.com.

A small building on the north side of the lodge served as the camp's business office. It was occupied by the manager and a secretary/bookkeeper. The cashier operated the front desk on the first floor of the lodge. Courtesy of the State Archives of Florida, *Florida Memory*, http://floridamemory.com.

The most prominent building on the ocean side of the fishing camp was the lodge. Encompassed by 12-foot-wide verandas, the first floor housed the lounge, front desk, and bathing rooms (see chapter 4). The second floor had guest rooms, a sitting room, and a writing room. The one-story building to the left of the lodge is the dining room. Circa 1912. Courtesy of the State Archives of Florida, *Florida Memory*, http://floridamemory.com.

A boardwalk ran between the east side of the lodge and the guest cottages up to the train station. The cottages were referred to as bungalows and were named after fish. Circa 1925. Courtesy of the Monroe County Public Library.

The stairs to the second floor of the lodge were outside on the north side, as shown in this circa 1912 image. Sabal palmetto trunks were used for columns on the porches of the lodge, the dining room, and some of the large bungalows. Known for their toughness and fire-resistance, the trunks were also sometimes used for wharf pilings. Courtesy of the Monroe County Public Library.

Except for days when the weather was cool, mosquitoes were a constant problem at the camp and discouraged guests from enjoying the lodge's verandas in the evenings. In later years, portions of the lodge's ground-floor verandas were screened. Circa 1933. Courtesy of Patricia J. Duane.

View inside the ground floor of the lodge looking toward the front desk and the northeast corner. The fixtures hanging from the ceiling are acetylene gas lamps. Courtesy of the State Archives of Florida, *Florida Memory*, http://floridamemory.com.

View looking toward the northwest corner of the lodge. The front desk is at the upper right. The desk lamp on the table in the foreground was also powered by acetylene gas. Courtesy of the State Archives of Florida, *Florida Memory*, http://floridamemory.com.

The southwest corner of the lounge as seen from the guest side of the front desk. The fireplace on the right was more than decorative; it warmed the lounge and was used most often during the cooler months of February and March. Courtesy of the State Archives of Florida, *Florida Memory*, http://floridamemory.com.

View looking toward the southeast corner of the lodge. The deer trophy may have been a key deer taken at Big Pine Key. Courtesy of the State Archives of Florida, *Florida Memory*, http://floridamemory.com.

A large work-camp bunkhouse was transformed into the dining room. The covered porch with sabal palmetto columns was added to enhance the entrance of the plain building. Guests were assigned to tables in a dining arrangement similar to that on a cruise ship. Circa 1923. Courtesy of the Wright Langley Archives.

George Schutt, manager of the camp, sits on the steps of his house. An unadorned wood-frame building, the Pompano was the only residential building other than the lodge to have a second floor. Circa 1930. Courtesy of Patricia J. Duane.

The Shark, situated just east of the lodge, was originally a construction crew bunkhouse that was renovated to provide eight single-guest rooms. Courtesy of the State Archives of Florida, *Florida Memory*, http://floridamemory.com.

The Tarpon was one of the smallest bungalows. It looks suspiciously like a recycled caboose. Courtesy of Patricia J. Duane.

The Porpoise was a small wood-frame bungalow. Courtesy of Patricia J. Duane.

The Dolphin, located east of the Shark, was also a former bunkhouse converted into eight single-guest accommodations. The large vent above the porch exhausted warm air from the rooms (*National Magazine*, April 1910).

The marina on the bay side of the Long Key Fishing Camp was a busy place for four months a year. Courtesy of the State Archives of Florida, *Florida Memory*, http://floridamemory.com.

The small building in the center of this photograph of the marina dock is the bait house, where live bait was kept in pens. To its right is the dockmaster's office. Yachts typically moored on the north side of the dock, and the camp's boats moored on the south side. Courtesy of the State Archives of Florida, *Florida Memory*, http://floridamemory.com.

People came to the Long Key Fishing Camp not only to fish, but to explore the adjacent islands and hunt. Two trap-shooting ranges were available at the camp to hone marksmanship. In this circa 1923 photograph, George Schutt awaits his turn. This five-station range (only three are visible) was located just west of the caretaker's cottage and south of the railroad embankment, which can be seen in the background through the palm trees. An arrow on the left side of the photograph points to the entrance to the small tunnel that passed through the embankment. Courtesy of the Wright Langley Archives.

The marina was closed during the off-season. The bait house and the dockmaster's office can be seen at the extreme left, while the gasoline storage tank is visible to their right onshore among the palm trees. The small building on the shore at the end of the dock is the taxidermist's workshop. The two large structures on the shore are the boat storage/maintenance buildings, in which all of the camp's boats were stored for eight months of the year. Courtesy of the Wright Langley Archives.

5

The Long Key Fishing Club

The appearance of the dolphin when just out of the water beggars description. Very few anglers in the world have ever had this experience. Not many anglers, perhaps, care for the beauty of a fish. But I do. And for the sake of those who feel the same way I wish I could paint him. But that seems impossible. For even while I gazed the fish changed color. He should have been called the chameleon of the ocean. He looked a quivering, shimmering, changeful creature, the color of golden-rod. He was the personification of beautiful color alive. The fact that he was dying made the changing hues. It gave me a pang—that I should be the cause of the death of so beautiful a thing.

If I caught his appearance for one fleeting instant here it is: vivid green-gold, spotted in brilliant blue, and each blue spot was a circle inclosing white. The long dorsal extending from nose to tail seemed black and purple near the head, shading toward the tail to rich olive green with splashes of blue. Just below the dorsal, on the background of gold, was a line of black dots. The fins were pearly silver beneath, and dark green above. All the upper body was gold shading to silver, and this silver held exquisite turquoise-blue spots surrounded with white rings, in strange contrast to those ringed dots above. There was even a suggestion of pink glints. And the eyes were a deep purple with gold iris.

The beauty of the dolphin resembled the mystery of the Gulf Stream—too illusive for the eye of man.

—Zane Grey, *Tales of Fishes*

The location of Long Key midway down the Florida Keys provided convenient access to a wide variety of game fish. Some such as bonefish were plentiful on the flats of Florida Bay and in the shallow water along the beach on the ocean side, and could be taken from the shore or in small boats. Tarpon frequented the channels between the islands and at night would come up to the marina dock and roll in the warm water. In forty-five minutes, one of the camp's boats could take a party to bottom-fish or troll near the living coral reef, the home for many different species that bordered the Florida Straits.[1]

Free of distractions, in a location with an abundance of fish of diverse varieties, and with comfortable accommodations and all the amenities a good fishing experience required, there was one thing the serious sportfisherman lacked at Long Key prior to the spring of 1912: the competitive challenge. This was addressed in March of that year, when Zane Grey and other guests of the camp formed the Long Key Fishing Club to recognize the taking of exceptional fish. The Long Key Fishing Club promptly awarded bronze, silver, and gold pins to thirty people, including Zane Grey, Isaac Guggenheim, and L. P. Schutt, based on fish taken at the camp.[2]

The Long Key Fishing Club was formally organized and its rules and objectives codified in March 1917. As stated in the *Long Key Fishing Club Booklet, Season 1934–35*, its purpose was: "to arouse among novices a keener interest in the art of angling by encouraging them to join and providing definite inducements and incentives, while keeping club fees small and requirements for prizes reasonable; to afford the skilled fisherman an unequalled opportunity for achieving the most difficult honors and for developing and perfecting in himself the finest features of the sport; and also to repress the wholesale killing of fish."

GOOD SPORTSMANSHIP Does Not Consist in **A BIG CATCH,**
But in The Use Of Light Tackle and a REASONABLE CATCH.
To Preserve The Species and To Keep This Place What it is Today—The Best Spot in Florida for Big Game Fish,
IT IS SUGGESTED That a Sportsman Should Limit Himself To

3 AMBERJACK
5 BARRACOUTA
2 SAIL FISH
5 TARPON
} **GAME FISH**

6 KING FISH
10 MACKEREL
6 GROUPER
} **FOOD FISH**

Any Fish Caught Above The Number Of Each Above Specified Should Be Carefully Returned To The Water.
PLAY Your Fish instead of **GAFFING** Him. Work For A "BUTTON" FISH.
RELEASE THE SMALL FISH.

This sign, reflecting the Long Key sportfishing ethos, hung on a wall near the front desk in the lodge, where guests were sure to see it when they checked in. Reproduced by Thomas Neil Knowles.

At the same meeting, specific rules for awards were approved, annual meetings were scheduled, and officers elected. Zane Grey was the first elected president of the club and served in that position for two seasons, 1917–18 and 1918–19.

Club pins, sometimes referred to as buttons, identified members and served as indicators of their level of achievement. Only members of the Long Key Fishing Club were entitled to possess and wear a club pin. Each member was given a bronze pin upon joining the club. Pins of silver, gold, and gold set with a diamond were awarded for landing fish of selected species that met the requirements for a given award category.

The rules for qualifying a catch included requirements regarding the type and strength of the tackle used to land the fish. A member could possess only one pin at a time. If a pin of higher value was awarded, the pin of lower value had to be returned.

As shown in this February 1923 photo, the official scale for weighing catches was located between the dockmaster's office and the bait house on the marina dock. Charter boats returned to the dock as quickly as possible after bringing aboard a potential record fish in order to minimize the dehydration and weight loss that could occur before the weigh-in. The pump at the left indicates that the camp sold Crown gasoline (see chapter 7 for more information on this brand). The gasoline was stored in a large tank onshore and gravity-fed to the pump. Courtesy of the Wright Langley Archives.

Table 5.1. Long Key Fishing Club award pins

Species	*Minimum qualifying weight (pounds)*		
	SILVER	GOLD	GOLD WITH DIAMOND
Tarpon	75	100	125
Sailfish or marlin	55	65	75
Kingfish	30	35	45
Amberjack	45	65	75
Wahoo	30	35	45
Permit	15	20	25
Bonefish	7	9	10

Source: *Long Key Fishing Club Booklet, Season 1934–35*.

The Long Key Fishing Club kept track of record catches taken by fishermen at the camp and published the names of record holders and the vital statistics of the catch in each season's edition of the club's brochure. Prizes of rods, reels, etc. were also awarded by the club. In addition to the fish for which pins were awarded, the club kept records on other species including Allison tuna, grouper, African pompano, dolphin, jack crevella, yellowtail, yellow jack, bonita, and cobia.

The Long Key Fishing Club belonged to its members and was technically independent of the Long Key Fishing Camp and the Florida East Coast Hotel Company. However, their mutually supportive relationship was acknowledged by the following statement in the club's annual booklet: "While it is not necessary to be a Club member to become a guest of the Camp, the Club has been highly instrumental in making the Long Key Fishing Camp the finest and most popular fishing resort in the world."[3]

The club set the standard for sportsmanship at the camp, and the Long Key ethos evolved. The explorer and sportsman Richard Sutton was impressed with the devotion of its practitioners and the penalty for noncompliance:

> At the majority of fishing resorts, angling is considered merely a life work. At Long Key it is looked upon as a religion. The majority of the visitors are old and hardened habitués, men who return to the club year after year, out of pure love for the sport. More skillful manipulators of the rod and reel I have never met. Woe betide the young enthusiast who pulls up alongside the dock at night with half a ton of fish, the majority of which have been snagged on elephantine tackle! He will not be openly censured, but it will be at least a month before he recovers from a severe case of chronic frostbite.[4]

The strong support of the goals of the club was aided by the long-term membership of sportsmen such as Zane Grey and B. W. Crowninshield, and by the consistent, mutually beneficial relationship maintained between the club and resort management. There were only two people who served as camp manager over the twenty-seven years the resort existed: L. P. Schutt and his oldest son, George. Both appreciated that much of the camp's fame and success derived from the membership of the club and that the club flourished because of the competitive environment encouraged by the camp's management. It was truly a symbiotic arrangement.

Table 5.2. Long Key Fishing Camp record fish

Catch	*Weight*	*Length*	*Season taken*	*Taken By*
WORLD RECORD				
Allison tuna[1]	132 lbs.		1933–34	Thomas Snyder
Kingfish[2]	59 lbs.	4' 11"	1925–26	Miss Mae Haines
CAMP RECORD[3]				
Barracuda	45 lbs.	4' 9"	1929–30	H. R. Mallinson
Bonefish	11 lbs. 3oz.		1926–27	Nat. Rogers
Cobia	82 lbs.		1929–30	Dr. R. E. Lee
Mangrove snapper	14 lbs.		1933–34	Miss Lucille Parsons
Permit	25 lbs. 9oz.		1924–25	A. F. Meisselbach
Sailfish	93 lbs.	7' 8"	1926–27	T.D.M. Cardeza
Tarpon	201 lbs.		1927–28	Mrs. W. Anderson
Wahoo	78 lbs.	5' 6"	1928–29	T.D.M. Cardeza
10-YEAR RECORD[4]				
African pompano	26 lbs.		1929–30	Harry Richman, C. K. McDowell
Amberjack	69 lbs.		1924–25	A. A. Hovell
Bonita	17 lbs.		1931–32	B. W. Crowninshield
Dolphin[5]	33 lbs.		1931–32	Col. H. C. Barthman
Grouper	51 lbs. 8oz.		1924–25	R. G. Hand
Jack crevella	28 lbs.		1929–30	R. M. Smith
Marlin	90 lbs.	7' 5"	1926–27	A. C. Ernest
Yellow jack	20 lbs.		1931–32	C. G. Schluederberg
Yellowtail	11 lbs.		1933–34	S. A. Kaufman

Source: Data from the *Long Key Fishing Club Booklet, Season 1934–35*, which did not include catches landed during 1935. That information would have appeared in the booklet for season 1935–36, had it been published.

Notes: 1. This Allison tuna was believed to be the Atlantic Ocean world record.

2. Kingfish are also referred to as king mackerel.

3. The camp record is for the duration of the camp's records.

4. The 10-year record is for seasons 1924–25 through 1933–34.

5. This fish is now known by the name mahimahi.

6

Sailfish and Boats

At Long Key the Gulf Stream is offshore five miles. The water shoals gradually anywhere from two feet near the beach to twenty feet five miles out on the reef.

. . . The Gulf Stream runs along the outer edge of the reef, and here between Tennessee Buoy and Alligator Light, eighteen miles, is a feeding-ground for sailfish, kingfish, amberjack, barracuda, and other fishes.

One day I found the Gulf Stream a mile off Tennessee Buoy, whereas on other days it would be close in. On this particular day the water was a dark, clear, indigo blue and appreciably warmer than the surrounding sea. This Stream has a current of several miles an hour, flowing up the coast. Everywhere we saw the Portuguese men-of-war shining on the waves. There was a slight, cool breeze blowing, rippling the water just enough to make fishing favorable. I saw a big loggerhead turtle, weighing about three hundred pounds, coming around on the surface among these Portuguese men-of-war, and as we ran up I saw that he was feeding on these queer balloon-like little creatures. Sometimes he would come up under one and it would stick on his back, and he would turn laboriously around from under it, and submerge his back so he had it floating again. Then he would open his cavernous mouth and take it in. Considering the stinging poison these Portuguese men-of-war secrete about them, the turtle must have had a very tabasco-sauce meal. Right away I began to see evidence of fish on the surface, which is always a good sign. We went past a school of bonita breaking the water up into little swirls. Then I saw a smashing break of a sailfish coming out sideways, sending the water in white sheets.

—Zane Grey, *Tales of Fishes*

Prior to 1916, large-game angling at Long Key primarily involved trolling for king mackerel and amberjack along the reef that formed the northwestern rim of the Florida Straits. Sailfish were plentiful, but they were almost impossible to catch. As if to torment the fisherman, a sailfish would swipe at a trolled bait with his bill and then show no further interest in the mangled mess on the hook as it was towed away by the boat. On other occasions sailfish would chew through the linen trolling line between the boat and the bait. In either case, valuable fishing time was lost while the line was reeled in and the ruined bait or the lost rig was replaced. Most charter-boat captains regarded the sailfish as a nuisance and tried to avoid them because the fish were so difficult to hook and often frustrated their clients.

The Atlantic sailfish can grow to a length of slightly more than 10 feet and reach a maximum weight of around 128 pounds. In the winter months they migrate north in vast schools that stretch for miles out in the Gulf Stream, where the current is strongest.[1]

Occasionally sailfish would come in close to the reef and would be snagged by a trolling boat. Then the fortunate fisherman was treated to a dazzling display of acrobatics, the fish dancing along the surface of the water on its tail, raising its sail and twisting to and fro as it tried to shake the hook loose. Sailfish have exceptional strength and endurance and are capable of making high-speed dashes, as fast as 68 mph, and deep dives, all of which present a challenge for even the most experienced sportfisherman. When properly prepared and mounted with its sail raised and menacing spear, the sailfish is often the most impressive trophy in an angler's collection. For these reasons, there was a continuing interest in finding a reliable method to induce sailfish to take trolled bait.

During the Long Key Fishing Camp's 1916 season, Zane Grey decided to try a trolling technique that he had heard was producing consistent catches of sailfish off Palm Beach and Miami. The idea was to make the bait mimic the behavior of stunned prey immediately after being struck by a sailfish's bill. This was accomplished by the angler operating his fishing reel in a certain manner so that the bait would go limp in the water and thereby entice the sailfish to take the drifting bait. Grey's trial run was a great success, and he shared the technique with boatmen and fishermen at the camp. At Long Key and elsewhere, this more effective trolling technique transformed the sailfish from a nuisance to a prized game fish.

The rapid rise in the popularity of the sailfish resulted in the camp's charter boats going farther out into the Florida Straits in search of the huge schools of sailfish. This created a dilemma for L. P. Schutt. When the camp began

The cabin cruiser *Dolphin* was one of several boats acquired by the camp from the fleet engaged in the construction of the viaduct. About 28 feet long, the boat was adequate for fishing along the reef, where the captain could quickly run into the sheltered water of Hawk Channel in the event of foul weather, but it lacked the freeboard and heft to safely ride the heavy seas that often occurred when fishing was best offshore in the Gulf Stream. Courtesy of Patricia J. Duane.

operation, it was provided with ten shallow-draft dories equipped with 3½-horsepower outboard motors for use on inshore waters and two surplus launches obtained from the Extension construction fleet for offshore fishing. The latter were motorized cabin cruisers with low sides in the area of the cockpit. The vessels were adequate for fishing near the reef, where Hawk Channel was close at hand and could provide sheltered water should the weather turn foul; however, when the boats ventured any distance out into the Gulf Stream, they were vulnerable to being swamped by the large swells that were often present when the fishing was best.[2]

L. P. Schutt brought this concern to the attention of the Florida East Coast Hotel Company management, and a contract was executed in 1919 with the Gibbs Gas Engine Company of Jacksonville for the design and construction of six cabin cruisers specifically for deepwater fishing.

Schutt worked closely with the designers, resulting in plans for a sturdy, no-frills day cruiser of seam batten V-bottom construction, with an overall length of 32 feet, a maximum width of 8 feet, and a draft of 2 feet, 4 inches. For ease of servicing and the stocking of spare parts, the boats were identical in every detail of construction and equipment. The hardware was of galvanized iron or brass, an important consideration in a salt-laden environment. An article published soon after the boats were placed in service indicates that Schutt's involvement produced a fleet of boats that were strong and functional.

> Following Mr. Schutt's requirements, the boats are simple, serviceable fishing craft without any sleeping accommodations. The guests at Long Key fishing camp, who will use these boats, spend only a few hours daily on board, and sleeping accommodations are provided at the camp. . . . No provision has been made for lighting other than by means of oil lamps for it is not expected that the boats will be used at night. . . . The specifications describe a sturdy, efficient type of boat, with the stem, stem knee, keel and deadwoods of white oak and the frames also of this material; seam battens and clamps of all heart yellow pine.

There were many features built into the new boats. A toilet was installed in a compartment at the forward end of the cabin. The forward deck and cockpit floor were covered with painted canvas providing a replaceable, nonslip surface. The cockpit was self-bailing, an essential safety feature in rough weather or when rinsing the deck after landing bleeding fish. There were two steering devices on board; a standard spoke-wheel helm mounted on the portside of the cabin bulkhead near the engine controls and a steering lever mounted on the starboard side of the cockpit. The lever allowed the captain to maneuver the boat with one hand while using his other hand to help bring the catch aboard. Brackets installed on the top of the forward deck securely held the anchor and an oar while allowing them to be readily accessible.[3]

Each boat was powered by a 20-horsepower inboard engine with an integrated transmission built by the Kermath Manufacturing Company of Detroit. The four-cylinder, four-cycle motor was mounted horizontally via a universal coupling that facilitated the removal and reinstallation of the engine. With a 20-inch, three-bladed propeller turning at 500–600 rpm, the boat could make a speed of 10 statute miles per hour.[4]

Named for famous Indian tribes, the six boats—the *Seminole, Apache, Iroquois, Huron, Aztec,* and *Mohican*—were delivered to the Florida East Coast Hotel Company at the builder's dock on the St. Johns River on December 17, 1919. They were turned over to Captain William "Bill" Uren and his team of boatmen from the camp for the 470-mile/six-day trip down the east coast of Florida to Long Key. L. P. Schutt was at the dock to greet them when they arrived just before Christmas.[5]

About seven weeks after the new boats arrived at the camp, one of them was chartered by Finley Barrell of Chicago, who invited his friend C. E. Lester to join him. Lester was in search of a record-setting sailfish, and his account of the trip provides a good description of the technique that Zane Grey had been promoting.

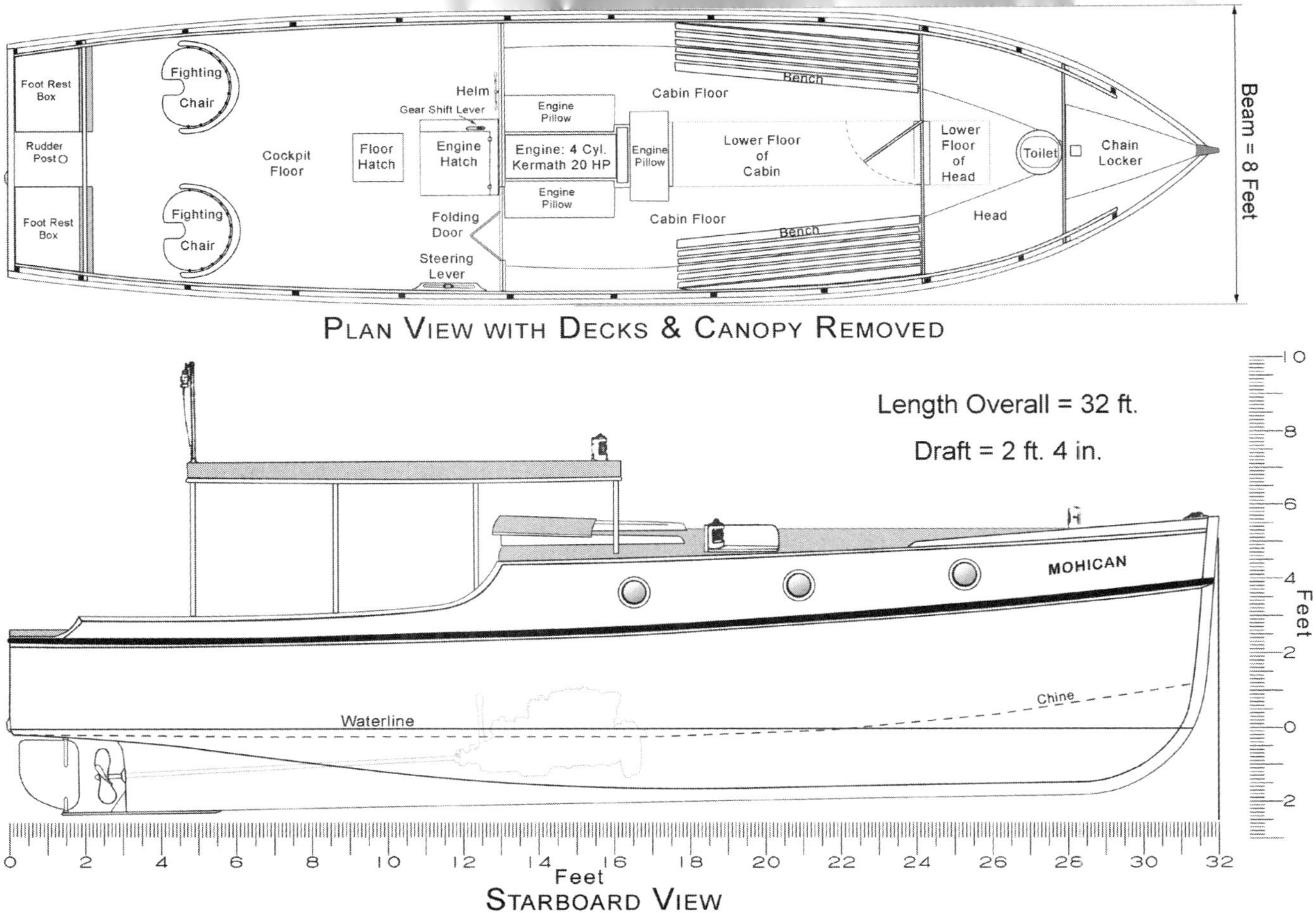

Plan for 32-foot cabin cruisers built for the Long Key Fishing Camp in 1919. Drawing by Thomas Neil Knowles based on a plan in *Motor Boat*, 1920.

The custom-built cabin cruisers arrived at Long Key just before Christmas 1919. In this photograph, the 32-foot cruisers dwarf one of the older boats tied up alongside. Courtesy of Patricia J. Duane.

A cold front had just moved through the Keys, generating long, deep swells offshore. The larger cabin cruiser with Captain Bill Uren at the helm safely rode the swells and pushed steadily along for 1½ hours until they were 8 miles out and in the deep, blue water of the Gulf Stream.

> Everything in readiness, at a word from Capt. Bill, we started to troll against the stream, the boat going about four miles an hour. We kept our bait about seventy-five to ninety feet astern. I found in fishing for sailfish it was best to have your bait just far enough away from the boat to keep it in sight all the time. After trolling a few minutes, Barrell had a "tap" but missed his fish. Shortly after, I had a "tap." Instantly I paid out about thirty feet of line. Then I waited for the line to straighten and struck hard, hooking the fish.
>
> In taking the bait, the fish rushes at it, making a side swipe at the bait, as if to kill it, then turns and swallows it. If after feeling the "tap" you move the bait, the fish will rarely take it. Hence the necessity for paying out the line for several yards after feeling the "tap." I believe one reason so many strikes from sailfish are missed is the fact that there is too much line out and one cannot watch the movement of the bait and fish.
>
> To "hark back," after setting the hook, out of the blue came a flash of silver, bronze and purple. The fish at once started to thrash along the surface of the water on its tail. It is rare that these fish jump clear of the water. They come to the surface rushing along for yards literally on their tails.[6]

After battling the fish for two hours and ten minutes, an exhausted Lester had his prize near the starboard side, where Uren had taken up station. With one hand the captain used the rudder lever to steer the boat to keep the fish alongside, while he reached out with the other hand in a heavy glove, grasped the sharp bill, and then brought the catch onboard. Two hours later, they were at the weigh station, where the sailfish was officially determined to be 7 feet 6 inches long and weigh 65 pounds, a new camp record for Atlantic sailfish on light tackle.

The next day, Lester, using even lighter tackle, went out again with Captain Uren and brought in another sailfish. Although this fish was slightly smaller (7 feet 5½ inches, and 51¾ pounds), Lester was told it had set a new world record for the lighter tackle.[7]

While the change in trolling technique and the new boats dramatically improved catches of sailfish, there was still some difficulty in attracting the fish to the trolled bait. This problem was overcome during the early 1920s when a guest from Philadelphia brought a new lure known as the "Tarporeno" to Long Key that seemed to be irresistible to sailfish.

The lure had multiple hooks dangling from its 8-inch body, a feature considered unsportsmanlike by the Long Key Fishing Club, so the boat captains removed them and used the stripped plug as a teaser. The removal of the hooks intensified the erratic motion of the body as it was trolled through the water, while its ivory-colored enamel tipped with a bright-red head made it highly visible. Richard Sutton described the teaser's action as being "like a demented water beetle that is suffering from an acute attack of paralysis agitans."[8]

Once a sailfish begins tracking the teaser, it is not long before he makes a run at the plug and takes a swipe at it. This is the cue for the boatman to begin withdrawing the decoy, moving it over the fishermen's baited hooks. By that time, the fish is so frustrated that he makes a strike at the bait.

The new boats, trolling techniques, and teasers greatly improved the odds of hooking sailfish and other large game fish, but one aspect of the sport greatly troubled Zane Grey and other big-game fishermen: namely, the use of heavy tackle, rigs, and lines that were so strong the hooked fish stood no chance of breaking them, and therefore no skill was required on the part of the angler to land him. Grey thought the practice not only unsportsmanlike, but a flagrant waste. "If fishermen will only study the use of light tackle they will soon appreciate a finer sport, more fun and gratification, and a saving of fish," he lamented.

He placed part of the blame on the boatmen for encouraging their clients to use heavy tackle:

> The trouble at Long Key is that new boatmen are hired each season, and, as they do not own their boats, all their interest centers in as big a catch as possible for each angler they take out, in the hope and expectation, of course, of a generous tip. Heavy tackle means a big catch and light tackle

> the reverse. And so tons of good food and game fish are brought in only to be thrown to the sharks. I mention this here to give it a wide publicity. It is criminal in these days and ought to be stopped.[9]

Grey was not alone in this crusade; other sportsmen such as Heilner, Lester, Cassiard, Crowninshield, Conill, Sutton, and the Schutts (L. P. and his son George) were advocates of the same view. Among the Long Key boatmen, Bill Uren and James L. Jordan were supporters of the light-tackle concept.

Jordan was so keen about the issue that in 1911 he founded the Cotton-Thread Fishing Club of America, which advocated the use of cotton thread instead of traditional high-strength linen line. When the stronger line is used, once the hook is set there is little doubt as to the capture of the fish. When cotton thread that will break under a strain of more than 3½ pounds is used, the contest has only begun when the fish is hooked. The angler must manipulate the rod and reel with great care the entire time, and the outcome remains uncertain until the fish is landed.[10]

The use of extremely light tackle requires more time to play the fish and results in smaller and fewer fish per trip than would otherwise be the case, a situation that light-tackle devotees gladly accept in return for the mental and physical challenge afforded by a more equal contest between man and fish. But even dedicated members of the Cotton-Thread Fishing Club of America such as Fred Ellsworth did not make a full-time commitment:

> Both Mrs. Ellsworth and myself were made honorary members of this unparalleled club, because of our use of light tackle for both fresh-water and big-game sea angling. Later I became an active member, and it was in 1916, while big game sea fishing at Long Key that we first used cotton thread. Both of us caught barracudas, dolphins and other fish, using Heddon six-foot bamboo bass rods, Meek No. 3 Bluegrass reels and 200 yards of Clark's O.N.T. No. 24 spool cotton thread, with fine copper wire leaders about a foot long, and 3/0 O. S. hooks baited with cut mackerel.
>
> Of course, that kind of equipment was out of place there when one has to pay $15.00 a day for a launch intended for sea fishing. But we only devoted a little time now and then to it for diversion, and it was all kinds of fun and sport.[11]

Not all of the clientele of the Long Key Fishing Camp were extremely wealthy people. Many of the guests who went there for the fishing stayed only a few days or a week at most and wanted, in return for the substantial outlay required for their visit, to catch as many big fish as possible.

7

The Clientele

> By those crossing from Havana, Long Key is regarded as an oasis where the travelers who have suffered from seasickness may stop to convalesce, lulled by the swish of cocoanut boughs, which movement resembles the sound of falling water. Long Key is reached just before coming to the great viaduct. The cabins cluster around the hotel, each one being named after a fish. The hotel itself is on a genuine "coral strand," and its pillars are of cabbage palms.
>
> The guests minutely inspected the signboards on each little cottage to be sure they were entering the right one; sometimes the name had a curious applicability to the occupant—a cadaverous money-lender emerged from a little house labelled "The Shark." A blooming orator, of ample proportions and rounded outlines, found a home at "The Porpoise," where he was permitted to sport to his heart's content. A lady owning a liberal supply of remarkably large and remarkably false-looking "store" teeth, was lodged in "The Barracoota," named after the only fish known to have teeth, a savage creature that has been known to snap off the legs of a child while bathing. Other names of fish displayed there are the kingfish, sawfish—in fact, every sort of seafish that I could think of except a sucker.
>
> —Mitchell Mannering, "The Hidden Wealth of Florida"

Richard Sutton's characterization of the Long Key Fishing Camp guests as being "old and hardened men" was not entirely accurate. They were a diverse lot of men and women that included entrepreneurs, politicians, businessmen, and aristocrats, young and old. Zane Grey, President Herbert Hoover, banker Andrew Mellon, and Charles Kettering, inventor of the automobile electric starter, were among the more prominent.

Franklin Delano Roosevelt visited Long Key several times during the mid-1920s, but he never stayed in the camp's accommodations or even went ashore. During the summer of 1921, at the age of thirty-nine, the future president of the United States became paralyzed from the waist down. The diagnosis was poliomyelitis, and he was told that the paralysis would be permanent. Fearing that being seen as a cripple would end his political career, he went to great lengths to avoid being photographed or appearing in public in his wheelchair or being seen carried up steps. Roosevelt did not accept that the paralysis was irreversible and was eager to find a therapy that would restore his ability to walk.[1]

The following March, after trying various medications and remedies without success, he decided to take a month-long cruise in the Florida Keys on a rented houseboat. Although fishing and swimming did not restore his ability to walk, he felt so good physically after the trip that he and a friend bought a used 71-foot houseboat and named it the *Larooco*.[2]

Roosevelt made cruises in the Florida Keys aboard the *Larooco* in 1924, 1925, and 1926, and he used Long Key as a base to receive mail and telegrams, and for provisioning and refueling. There is no record of him going ashore or

Augustus (Gus) F. Meisselbach and his wife were regular guests at Long Key. He and his brother designed and manufactured fishing reels in Newark, New Jersey, for several decades. Gus was an expert at bonefishing. He is the only guest known to have hooked a sailfish and reeled in a 12-foot shark, all on the same bait. Courtesy of Patricia J. Duane.

Franklin Delano Roosevelt (*right*) "bathing" in the shallow water at the Long Key Fishing Camp beach, circa 1925. After he was stricken with polio, FDR made several trips to the Florida Keys and Long Key. Courtesy of the Franklin D. Roosevelt Presidential Library and Museum, Hyde Park, New York.

lodging at the camp. One of Roosevelt's entries in the vessel's log read: "April 5, 1924 . . . went round to the Ocean side of Long Key and had a fine 'bathe' in shallow water—sharks playing outshore from us." Another entry noted the high price of gasoline: "February 18, 1925 . . . Went to Long Key dock for gas—which we found was 34¢ though only 26¢ in Maine."[3]

The higher price of gasoline sold at the marina may have been due in part to the successful breakup of Standard Oil's monopolistic hold on the petroleum industry. In 1911, the U.S. Supreme Court ordered Standard dismantled into thirty-three separate companies. After the dust settled, the Long Key Fishing Camp obtained gasoline from Standard Oil of Kentucky, which was the distributor for Kentucky, Florida, Georgia, Alabama, and Mississippi. They marketed their gasoline using the brand name "Crown Gasoline," a knockoff of the pre-1911 Standard Oil "Red Crown" brand. Standard Oil of Kentucky was strictly a middleman with no production or refining facilities and had to purchase its gasoline from Standard of New Jersey, which added to the markup. Another factor that increased the cost was that the camp's gasoline was brought in by barge.[4]

In March 1929, New York Yankee slugger Lou Gehrig stayed at Long Key as the guest of N. Jerlaw, a Chicago attorney and expert light-tackle fisherman. Gehrig was a teammate of Babe Ruth and was one of the stars on the New York Yankees team that had won the World Series the previous two years. The twenty-five-year-old first baseman proved to be just as adept on the water as on the playing field and caught a 55-pound amberjack, a season record for the Long Key Fishing Club.

In March 1934, newlywed Gehrig reeled in a 7-foot sailfish while his wife matched his catch of tarpon, four apiece. That summer Gehrig, who was known as the "Iron Horse" because of his durability as a baseball player, collapsed during a ball game and had to be helped off the field. The incident was described as a lumbago attack. He continued to play baseball and had one of his best seasons.

Lou Gehrig made his final visit to Long Key in March 1935. Catches during the visit included a 6-foot, 9-inch sailfish as well as dolphin, kingfish, and mackerel. He had become an enthusiastic light-tackle advocate and fished with his friend from Chicago whenever he could. Jerlaw, a world light-tackle sailfishing champion, thought the athlete showed great promise in mastering featherweight tackle.

On Gehrig's last day at the Long Key Fishing Camp, he and Jerlaw went fishing together for sailfish with extremely lightweight tackle. To their surprise, a large manta ray approached their boat, swimming just beneath the surface. The magnificent animal was estimated to be 18–20 feet across and to weigh about 2,000 pounds. As if sensing that the men could do him no harm, the fish leisurely crossed their wake, slipping under the fishing lines that were being trolled. Gehrig noted the irony of the situation later when he told a reporter: "Of course, we couldn't have bothered this fellow, no matter what outfits we had had unless they had been harpoons, but it was certainly incongruous for us to be out there with the lightest deep-sea tackle in the world when we sighted this giant." He added, "My real thrill this time was seeing that manta."[5]

For some guests it was not marine life that kept them returning to the Long Key Fishing Camp. Such was the case of poet and businessman Wallace Stevens, who began visiting Long Key in 1922. During his student days, Stevens aspired to a literary career, and by the end of his junior year at Harvard he had won all of the university's writing awards. Unable to finish at Harvard due to

Lou Gehrig, also known as the "Iron Man of Baseball," married Eleanor Twitchell in September 1933 and took her to Long Key the next March. Here the New York Yankee first baseman and his bride pose with a 7-foot sailfish Gehrig landed. The couple also caught four tarpon apiece, and Eleanor brought aboard several dolphin. The man on the right is N. Jerlaw, a close friend of the Gehrigs. Courtesy of Patricia J. Duane.

financial problems, he subsequently earned a law degree from the New York School of Law and was admitted to the New York Bar in 1904. In 1908, he began a highly successful forty-seven-year career in the insurance industry, where he rose through the ranks of management to an executive position. Throughout his professional endeavors, Stevens continued to pursue his literary avocation.[6]

At the time of his first trip to the Long Key Fishing Camp, Stevens was head of the bonds and surety department at the Hartford Accident and Indemnity Company. A large, well-proportioned man forty years of age, he was finishing his first major book of poetry, and his poems and plays were drawing praise from critics and literary circles when his professional duties took him to Florida.

After the end of the Great War in 1918, automobile ownership increased dramatically and sparked an insatiable demand for paved roads. The Hartford and other insurance companies became actively involved in Florida's burgeoning highway-construction program. Among other projects, the Hartford was

Left: Chicago attorney N. Jerlaw. Jerlaw, a camp regular, always reserved the same room on the second floor of the west side of the lodge, where he could sit in his rocking chair on the veranda and watch the sunset behind the Long Key Viaduct. This photograph of him on the second-floor veranda was taken from the roof of the breezeway that connected the lodge to the dining hall. *Right*: Photograph bearing Buck Duane's inscription "N. Jerlaw's Long Key Headquarters" with an arrow indicating his room. Courtesy of Patricia J. Duane.

the surety for a firm involved in building a highway known as the Tamiami Trail between Tampa and Miami. The Hartford's practice was to have outside law firms handle the processing of claims, with Stevens and his staff conferring with them as needed and approving the final settlement.

Many of the cases arising in the Southeast were assigned to law firms in Atlanta. Stevens had set up the Tamiami Trail firm's construction bond and in the early 1920s was called upon to travel during the winter to Atlanta and Florida to deal with various legal matters. In so doing, he developed a network of business friends.

In early January 1922, Stevens and an Atlanta associate, Judge Arthur Powell, were in Miami working out a settlement. Powell encouraged Stevens to stay at Long Key while the final agreement was being prepared for his signature. He did so and found the several days spent at the fishing camp to be a very enjoyable experience. Later in the month, while in Washington, D.C., Stevens was invited by Judge Powell to go down to Long Key again, this time in a private railroad car with a group of influential men that included the governor of Georgia and the president of a Georgia short-line railroad. Stevens joined them in Jacksonville, and the party began.

Stevens had an appetite for alcohol that matched his large size. He wrote to a friend that while at the fishing camp he became a charter member of the "Long Key Fishing Club of Atlanta" and that the "initiation" took three days and only two cases of scotch.

Henry Flagler, who drank in moderation, had insisted that all his hotels serve alcohol. In 1920, seven years after his death, Congress enacted the Volstead Act, a law that prohibited the manufacture or sale of liquor in the United States, resulting in the bars at Long Key and other Florida East Coast Hotel Company facilities in Florida being closed from 1920 to 1930, a period that became known as the Prohibition Era.

Liquor smuggling was commonplace all along the east coast and in the Florida Keys; guests seeking an alcoholic drink could obtain the makings without much difficulty. Stevens and his party did not have to rely on local smugglers, thanks in part to Henry Flagler. The railroad car in which the group traveled and took their meals had been built for Flagler and had been acquired by the father of the president of the short-line railroad after Flagler's death. Its ample liquor locker had been well stocked in Georgia.

This photograph of insurance man Wallace Stevens was taken in the spring of 1922, not long after he made his first trip to Long Key. Stevens also wrote poetry as a sideline and won the Pulitzer Prize for his work in 1955. A heavy drinker, he reportedly could become obnoxious when intoxicated and had run-ins with Robert Frost and Hemingway during the 1930s. Although he was not a sportfisherman, Wallace Stevens was a regular guest at the Long Key Fishing Camp from 1922 to 1935. Thomas Neil Knowles Collection.

Although not a sportfisherman, Stevens went fishing with his comrades during the day to be sociable. He was especially impressed with the vivid colors, describing them to his wife as the "yellow green cocoanut palms," and "the sky brilliantly clear and intensely blue, the sea blue and green beyond what you have ever seen." In the evenings, the poet sought out a quiet place where he could enjoy the view of the moonlit beach and be alone.

The paradisiacal environment made Long Key special for him. He wrote to his wife of the enjoyment he derived from being free to get up early in the morning and go for a swim in just his pajamas, adding for her peace of mind that there were no ladies present so he felt free to do as he pleased. The laid-back atmosphere of the fishing camp released Stevens from the stifling protocols of the insurance business, the mild weather freed him from the physical confinement imposed by the cold New England winter, and the natural beauty and quietness made inhibitions irrelevant and gave the poet a sanctuary for introspection and creative reflection. It is no wonder that for the next thirteen years Wallace Stevens ensured that each winter his business took him to south Florida and allowed him time to return to Long Key.[7]

It is likely that Stevens did encounter women and possibly children on some of his subsequent visits. The Long Key Fishing Club's booklet made clear that the resort and club were not exclusively for men, declaring, "It is an ideal resort for men, women and children, and a place where families are welcomed and women are eligible to Club membership."[8]

A most intriguing woman was elected to membership in the Long Key Fishing Club at the March 1931 meeting. Marguerite "Daisy" Hyde Leiter was born in Chicago in 1879. Her father, Levi Leiter, was a dry-goods millionaire who cofounded the Leiter & Field department store that later became known as Marshall Field's. She had a brother and two sisters.

Leiter's three daughters married British subjects. In 1895, Daisy's older sister, Mary, married George Curzon, an ambitious man of noble lineage and modest means for whom the marriage provided much-needed financial support. In 1898, he was appointed "Viceroy of the Indian Empire" and awarded the title Baron Curzon of Kedleston; Mary became Lady Curzon. While visiting Mary in India, Daisy and her sister Nancy met British officers, to whom they were wed in 1904.

Daisy's husband, Henry Molyneux Paget Howard, had become the 19th Earl of Suffolk and 12th Earl of Berkshire when his father died in 1898. Upon marrying Henry, Daisy became the Countess of Suffolk and Berkshire. The couple had three sons: Charles Henry George Howard, Cecil John Arthur Howard, and Greville Reginald Howard. The family lived at Charlton Park,

Malmesbury, England, in a manor completed in 1607 for the Earl and Countess of Suffolk.[9]

After their wedding, Henry and Daisy traveled extensively, frequently to India, and went on safaris in Africa. Tall and slim, the countess was adventurous and shared with her husband a love of fast cars and the recently invented flying machine called the airplane.

Lord Suffolk was a major in the Royal Field Artillery during the Great War and commanded the B/Fifty-Sixth Battery in the Mesopotamian Campaign. In April 1917, at the Battle of Istabulat about 45 miles northwest of Baghdad, a piece of shrapnel pierced his heart, killing the thirty-nine-year-old nobleman. Upon his father's death, his eldest son, Charles, who had just celebrated his eleventh birthday, became the 20th Earl of Suffolk and the 13th Earl of Berkshire. Since the title "countess" was reserved for the wife of the earl, Daisy's official title changed to the Dowager Countess of Suffolk and Berkshire, although she continued to be referred to as the countess.[10]

When Daisy's father died in 1904, he left $30 million to his heirs in a trust managed by her brother, Joseph. Subsequently her sister Mary and her mother

In this mid-1920s photograph, George Schutt (*extreme right*) watches new arrivals as he chats with a staff member believed to be John Scribner, the caretaker at that time. Guests of the Long Key Fishing Camp included men, women, and entire families with children and nannies. Courtesy of the Wright Langley Archives.

This photograph of the Countess of Suffolk and Berkshire was taken around 1910–15, when she was in her thirties. A Chicagoan whose maiden name was Marguerite "Daisy" Hyde Leiter, she was an heiress of a multimillionaire merchant and coal operator. Courtesy of the Library of Congress.

died. In 1923, Daisy with Mary's children initiated a lawsuit to have Joseph removed as trustee, citing incompetence and extravagance in managing the Leiter trust. Her sister Nancy sided with Joseph but died a year before the case was decided, leaving just Joseph and Daisy the surviving original beneficiaries. After eight years of litigation, the appellate court upheld Joseph as the trustee. Vindicated, he promptly resigned the position and died the following year, making Daisy the only living original beneficiary of the Leiter trust.[11]

Levi Leiter had stipulated in his will that in order for Daisy to receive her inheritance she had to live at least four months of every year in the United States. After her husband died, she began spending winters in Tucson, Arizona, and built homes in that state over a period of years. Her passion for excitement undiminished, she continued to go on safaris, maintained her interest in airplanes, and discovered the thrill of sportfishing.[12]

When she first visited Long Key is not known, but she was elected to membership in the Long Key Fishing Club in March 1931. Also joining the club at that time was a retired British army officer, Lt. Col. E. S. Gillett, a gentleman who newspaper accounts indicate was a companion of the countess as early as 1921. Although listed separately in the membership section of the club's booklet for the 1931 season, the countess and Gillett gave the same address (Charlton Park, Malmesbury, England) as their residence.[13]

At about the time she became a member of the club, the countess had a house built at the Long Key resort for $25,000 (approximately equivalent to $377,000 in 2012) that would comfortably accommodate her and Lieutenant Colonel Gillett as well as guests and servants. From the outside, the building was similar in appearance to several other large bungalows, but inside it was filled with objects d'art and fine furnishings. A spacious, stand-alone, circular shower house was constructed on the beach near the house. The countess's bungalow was named the "Wahoo" in keeping with the custom of naming the resort's cottages after fish.[14]

In 1932, the countess left her mark in the Long Key Fishing Club's record book by landing a 65-pound tarpon. Although it was the largest taken during the season, the fish was 10 pounds under the minimum to qualify for an award pin. In 1934, the 55-year-old countess caught the largest sailfish landed during the season, a 6-foot, 7-inch specimen weighing 40 pounds, but missed qualifying for a silver pin by 15 pounds; however, Gillett brought home a gold pin for landing a 106-pound tarpon, the record tarpon for the season.[15]

Two other members of the Long Key Fishing Club had large bungalows for their exclusive use in the 1930s. They were Benjamin ("Benny") Williams Crowninshield and Thomas Drake Martinez Cardeza.

The Wahoo was a large bungalow built for the Countess of Suffolk around 1930. Of quality construction throughout, its foundation piers were of concrete instead of the wood piles used in other bungalows. It had electrical service, most likely provided by its own generator. Courtesy of Patricia J. Duane.

The Bonefish (*foreground*) and its neighbor, the Marlin, were originally work-camp bunkhouses that were renovated so that each contained eight, single-guest rooms. By the 1930s they had been renovated into spacious bungalows for the exclusive use of certain patrons. The Bonefish was reserved for the Thomas M. Cardeza family of Philadelphia, while the Marlin was reserved for Benjamin Williams Crowninshield of Boston. Courtesy of Patricia J. Duane.

Crowninshield (1871–1953) was one of four children born to a wealthy Boston merchant, Benjamin W. Crowninshield, and his wife, the former Katherine M. Bradlee. His great-grandfather Benjamin Williams Crowninshield was a member of Congress from Massachusetts (1811–12) and served as secretary of the Navy from 1815 to 1818. The Crowninshields were one of the exclusive First Families of Boston, whose members trace their lineage to the founders of the city and the early settlers of New England. Considered to be one of the historic core families of the East Coast establishment, the Crowninshields were wealthy, politically powerful, and socially elite, and tended to marry into similarly ranked families. Benny's brother, Francis Boardman Crowninshield, also known as Frank Crowninshield and "Kino," married Louise du Pont in 1900.[16]

Benny Crowninshield attended Harvard from 1890 to 1894, but never completed his degree. A shrewd investor, he made a fortune in the stock market. Described by a family member as "short and colorless," he dressed tastefully without being ostentatious, was mild-mannered, and never married. When asked for his home address, Benny always responded with 164 Marlborough Street in Boston, the mansion his father built. This he did even after he became fed up with Massachusetts's taxes and made Boca Grande on Florida's west coast his legal domicile. He spent the winter and spring in Florida and summers in Massachusetts.

B. W. Crowninshield joined the Long Key Fishing Club in its early years and was a member of a select group of dedicated sportfishermen at the fishing camp that included Zane Grey. Grey christened the clique "The Bonefish Brigade" and immortalized the anglers in a satirical article of the same name published in 1922.[17]

The third guest of the camp who had a bungalow reserved for his exclusive use was Thomas Drake Martinez Cardeza (1875–1952). Cardeza was the only child of a Philadelphia lawyer and the heiress to the Thomas Drake fortune. A sportsman and explorer, his primary occupation was serving as a director of the Fidelity Trust Company, a Philadelphia bank his maternal grandfather had helped to establish. When he was about forty, he married Mary Racine (1880–1943), who was born in France and is a descendant of the seventeenth-century French dramatist Jean Racine.[18]

Cardeza's wealth derived from Thomas Drake (1807–1890), a pioneer in the manufacture of denim clothing who invested wisely and accumulated substantial holdings in banks, insurance companies, and railroads. When he died in 1890, he left a Philadelphia mansion and $5 million to his only child, Charlotte.[19]

Charlotte Wardle Drake (1854–1939) married James Warburton Martinez Cardeza (1855–1932) when she was twenty years old and he was nineteen. The next year she gave birth to their son, Thomas. At age thirty-six, Charlotte inherited her father's estate. She took up big-game hunting and was said to be an excellent shot. Her son accompanied her on most of her adventures.[20]

She bought the *Eleanor* in 1898, a yacht reputed at that time to be "the finest vessel for pleasure ever constructed in America." Charlotte Cardeza became the first woman to circumnavigate the earth in her own yacht, although the feat did not involve much in the way of hardship. The luxuriously appointed ship was almost as long as a football field and had a crew of forty, including a physician and a gourmet chef. After another trip around the globe and other voyages, she sold the yacht in 1900. That year she divorced her husband of twenty-six years because of his alleged involvement in an affair. She favored being called "Lady Cardeza" based on the claim that her former husband's grandfather had been a Spanish don.[21]

Returning from a safari in 1912, she booked one of the two most expensive suites of the RMS *Titanic* on its tragic maiden voyage. She, her son, his manservant, and her maid all survived the sinking of the liner, although there

Millionaires' Beach would have been an appropriate name for this stretch of oceanside shoreline at the east end of the camp. The Cardezas' Bonefish is on the left; Benny Crowninshield's Marlin is in the center; and the Wahoo, belonging to the Dowager Countess of Suffolk and Berkshire, is at the far right. Courtesy of Patricia J. Duane.

were some reports that bribery was involved in saving the men. Her claim of $117,352, which included $30,000 in jewelry, was the largest filed against the ship's owners.[22]

When the Cardezas first visited Long Key is not known, but Thomas was there during the 1926–27 season and caught a 7-foot, 8-inch sailfish weighing 93 pounds, a camp record. It earned him the Long Key Fishing Club's highest award, a gold pin set with a diamond. Both he and his wife remained members of the club and were regular guests at the fishing camp until its destruction.[23]

So it was that even at Long Key there was a distinction between the wealthy and the very wealthy, with the latter having the largest bungalows located closest to the beach reserved the entire season for their exclusive use.

8

The Staff

One of the most important branches of the hotel business is the conduct of resort hotels. Some of these, like the houses at Lakewood, Atlantic City, Old Point Comfort and the Hot Springs of Arkansas, are open all the year. But the greater number are short season houses—the summer months in the North, the winter months in the South. Many of the Jersey, Long Island and Florida coast hotels are open only two or three months in twelve. Mammoth houses like those at Long Beach, St. Augustine, Palm Beach, Saratoga and Tampa, must be filled during the season or a fortune is lost. Many proprietors of short season houses run two hotels, one at a summer resort, and the other at a winter resort in one of the large cities. So great is the number of resort hotels on the Atlantic Coast, that it might be possible for persons cruising on a yacht from Bar Harbor to Key West, to put in-shore at random every night, and sleep at a great inn. . . . Where the proprietor owns two resort hotels, he usually transfers his employees in a body, from one to the other, for their respective seasons. Most of the resort hotels are run on the American plan, and, in good seasons, the profits are large.

—Gilson Willets, *Workers of the Nation*

Since the Long Key Fishing Camp was owned by a corporation, it was the manager's role to represent the owner's interests and to see to the safety, welfare, and satisfaction of the guests. The manager, like most people making a living solely from seasonal resort work, had a nomadic lifestyle. From December to

April, L. P. Schutt and his family were at the camp, where they resided in the Pompano, a relatively spacious, two-story bungalow located near the train station. When the season at Long Key ended, the Schutts traveled north 1,500 miles to the mountains of Greene County, New York, where they had their home, and L. P. managed a resort from June to November. While away from the Florida Keys, the manager kept the fishing camp's reservation ledger with him; advertisements for the camp included a telegraph address so that guests could contact him and make reservations during the off-season.

As experienced as Schutt was, he could not foresee all exigencies. A good example is an incident that occurred during the Great War era, when one of the camp's boat captains reported that an errant naval mine had washed up on a sandbar near the reef. Immediately recognizing the danger posed by the explosive device should it be moved back into the water by a high tide and make contact with one of the camp's fishing boats, Schutt arranged for the mine to be retrieved and notified the authorities. In a letter dated March 4, 1917, he informed Maj. E. B. Martindale Jr. of the Coast Artillery Corps of the cost of recovering the explosive device.

> Capt. E. W. Putney reached Long Key to-day to take in charge the mine of which I wrote you about. He will no doubt be back with it by the time this reaches you. Was glad to be able to turn this over to him and if the Government gives any remuneration would leave it to them as to what they deem fit to offer. To procure the mine, I gave two launch men $5 to go out 8 or 10 miles to this sand bar on which the mine was located, and bring it in.

The letter made its way through the federal bureaucracy and ended up at the U.S. Treasury. On August 3, 1917, the comptroller of the United States, Walter W. Warwick, advised the secretary of war of his decision not to authorize reimbursement of the five-dollar retrieval cost for the following reasons:

> The mine had been washed up on the sand bar; it was not drifting in the open sea; so far as appears it was no longer apparently in danger of drifting again into the open sea and going beyond the control of its proper owners. There was seemingly no hazard incurred in its recovery and delivery to the military authorities. It seems to me, under these circumstances, it partakes merely of the nature of finding lost property rather than of the nature of salvage.
>
> The action of Mr. Schutt was public spirited and meritorious, but it did not create a legal obligation against the United States, and I am of opinion that payment of the claim is not authorized by law.[1]

The money paid the men to retrieve the mine was most likely written off as an expense of maintaining the camp.

For more than a decade Schutt's attention to detail, genuine concern for the well-being of guests, and congenial personality helped the Long Key Fishing Camp mature into a world-renowned resort with an elite clientele. This did not go unnoticed by the management of the Florida East Coast Hotel Company when they built the Flagler system's last resort.

Henry Flagler had intended to build a resort in Key West, but he did not live to see the project come to fruition. In 1914, a year after his death, the decision was made to honor his intention and planning was begun. The plans were drawn by the same architects who designed the New York City Metropolitan Opera House, the New York Public Library, and the U.S. Senate and House of Representatives office buildings in Washington, D.C.; however, construction was delayed. With work still under way on the railroad (including the replacement of temporary trestles erected so that the ailing Flagler could ride the first train to Key West) and the disruption of the Great War, it was 1918 before the company acquired a 13-acre site on the south side of Key West and commenced construction of the Casa Marina Hotel. The tract included 2,000 feet of shoreline on the ocean side of the island.

L. P. Schutt with his sons on the Long Key marina dock in 1920. *Left to right*: Peter, L. P., George with his dog, and Frank Schutt. Courtesy of the State Archives of Florida, *Florida Memory*, http://floridamemory.com.

The Casa Marina opened in Key West on New Year's Eve 1921 under the management of L. P. Schutt. It was the city's premier hotel for many years. Located on a rocky stretch of shore on the ocean side of the island, the hotel's broad beach was created with many tons of imported sand. Courtesy of the State Archives of Florida, *Florida Memory*, http://floridamemory.com.

The hotel was of Mediterranean architecture and constructed of reinforced concrete so that it could withstand any hurricane. The resort boasted four hundred guest rooms, a spacious ballroom, a large dining room, and a kitchen manned by world-class chefs. Because it was more than a mile from the rail yard, freshwater for the facility could not be hauled in by train, so eight cavernous, concrete cisterns that could store 750,000 gallons of rainwater were built under the dining room, ballroom, and lobby. On the exterior, immaculately groomed grounds wrapped around the buildings and recreational facilities that included tennis and shuffleboard courts. The rocky shoreline was transformed into a superb beach by hauling in many tons of sand. A sturdy pier projecting from the beach was available for fishing and for boarding charter boats.[2]

The Casa Marina represented a significant investment by the Florida East Coast Hotel Company, and an experienced hand was needed to manage the fledgling resort. L. P. Schutt was tapped for the job. Although the Casa Marina was a year away from its formal opening, the *Catskill Recorder* reported in December 1920 that L. P. and his wife were leaving Greene County, New York, for Key West, where he was to be manager of the Casa Marina, and that his son George G. Schutt and his family were going to Long Key, where George was taking over as manager. For several years thereafter, L. P. was listed in advertisements as the manager of both the Casa Marina and the Long Key Fishing Camp, although articles in various media indicate his son was actually managing the Long Key resort.[3]

George Schutt had worked for the Florida East Coast Hotel Company in the Bahamas, where he had been under the tutelage of H. E. Bemis before coming to Long Key and working for his father. In the 1920 census, he was listed as the Long Key Fishing Camp's cashier. A congenial host like his father, George was an accomplished fisherman well-respected by the Long Key sportfishing community. In 1925, Hamilton Wright wrote in the *Brooklyn (N.Y.) Daily Eagle*, "This is the third season that I have fished at Long Key, and George Schutt, of whom Zane Grey has spoken as one of the greatest of fishermen and who knows the lore of fishing and the habits of these speed demons of the gulf stream [sailfish] as few men know them, was with me."[4]

Late in December 1925, it was George's turn to deal with an unusual problem, one that only the wealthy could have. Office-machine magnate Albert B. Dick of Chicago, his wife, and their guests had departed Palm Beach aboard his luxurious houseboat for a leisurely holiday cruise through the Florida Keys. On Christmas Day, Dick gave his wife a $25,000 marquis

George Schutt succeeded his father as manager of the Long Key Fishing Camp in 1920 and remained in that position for fifteen years. He was fifty-two years old when the Long Key Fishing Camp was destroyed by a hurricane. An expert fisherman and competent hotel manager, he preferred knickers and a bow tie for informal wear. Courtesy of Patricia J. Duane.

diamond-and-platinum bracelet. The next morning, the party stopped at the Long Key Fishing Camp and went ashore for a brief visit. As she returned to the houseboat, Mrs. Dick slipped on the gangway and struck her arm against a stanchion. The blow broke the band of her bracelet and the bejeweled piece slipped off her wrist and into the water.

Since the water was only 7 feet deep, the bracelet's retrieval was expected to be a minor inconvenience. Without delay, one of the houseboat's crew donned a diving mask and went into the water, but he was unsuccessful in his search. Repeated dives and even night dives using powerful lights did not yield the glittering band. After an unplanned week's stay without recovering the bracelet, Dick announced a substantial reward for its return, and he and his party headed back to Palm Beach.

Rumors began to circulate that the shiny diamond-encrusted piece had been swallowed by a barracuda or grouper. Soon the location where the houseboat had been moored was besieged by fishermen. The most unusual fishing contest ever to occur at the Long Key Fishing Camp was to end without a declared winner; the bracelet was never reported to have been found.[5]

One of the most important responsibilities of the manager was ensuring that visitors to the camp were given appropriate attention and that those with outstanding catches received fitting recognition. This was especially critical when members of the Long Key Fishing Club were involved. One of George Schutt's most challenging incidents in this regard involved a sitting president of the United States.

Herbert Hoover began visiting Long Key in 1924, while he was secretary of commerce (1921–28). His most impressive visit occurred in 1930, one year after he was elected president. Determined to catch a trophy sailfish, Hoover scheduled a ten-day vacation in February to fish the Florida Keys out of Long Key. The visit became a mammoth production involving Secret Service personnel, a private railroad car, Department of Commerce tenders, Coast Guard cutters, and a chartered fleet that included a palatial yacht and smaller boats for fishing and courier service.

Since the Long Key Fishing Camp would serve as the base of operations, manager George Schutt was kept busy coordinating with the Secret Service on security matters and with the telephone company on the installation of a dedicated telephone line connecting the Long Key dock directly to the White House. In addition, he had to follow up with his staff to ensure appropriate accommodations were reserved for the president's shore party and that arrangements had been made for the delivery and storage of provisions and fuel to support the vessels.[6]

President Herbert Hoover (*left*) invited U. S. Supreme Court Justice Harlan F. Stone (*right*) to go on a fishing trip with him at Long Key in February 1930. The wives of both men went with them. Hoover wanted dearly to catch a trophy sailfish, but it was Justice Stone's wife, Agnes, who caught the largest sailfish and was awarded a prestigious Long Key Fishing Club gold pin. Courtesy of the Library of Congress.

Before dawn on Monday, February 10, 1930, the Havana Special arrived about four hours earlier than its normal schedule at the Long Key station and a private car was uncoupled and shunted onto a siding. As soon as it was light, President and Mrs. Hoover emerged from the car and were greeted by an impromptu gathering of people staying at the camp. The Hoovers were joined by their guests: U.S. Supreme Court Justice Harlan F. Stone and his wife, Agnes; writer and newspaperman Mark Sullivan and his wife; and Dr. Vernon Kellogg. Without pause or ceremony, the presidential party walked to the large dock at the marina where the yacht *Saunterer* was tied up. Described as a "seagoing houseboat," the 98-foot-long vessel was almost brand-new, having been built in 1928 for Jeremiah Milbank, a banker who had served as treasurer of the GOP when Hoover was elected.[7]

Moored nearby was the Department of Commerce motor vessel *Kilkenny*, a former yacht acquired by the department in 1917 for coastal patrols. Officially listed as a lighthouse tender, the 80-foot-long vessel had been renovated to augment and improve its accommodations. During the eight years he was secretary of commerce, Hoover had used the vessel for working vacations, sometimes taking his family along. The mission of the *Kilkenny* on this occasion was to carry one of the president's secretaries and his wife, the White House physician, and clerical staff.[8]

The president, Mrs. Hoover, and their guests boarded the *Saunterer*. After breakfast, the vessels got under way and rendezvoused with two Coast Guard cutters, another Department of Commerce tender, and six chartered small craft. The entire flotilla then moved to an area near the first site to be fished, where the large vessels anchored. Some of the small craft came alongside the *Saunterer*, picked up their parties, and then headed out for a day's fishing. This procedure was repeated during the trip, with the fleet moving to new locations ranging from Sombrero Reef south of Marathon to Alligator Reef south of Islamorada.[9]

The president and his guests did not set foot ashore for six days, using the yacht as their floating hotel and the small boats for fishing expeditions. This arrangement enabled them to maximize fishing time and kept them well away from mosquitoes. It also assured their privacy since newsmen covering the trip were not allowed to accompany the vessels and were left behind at Long Key. The president's staff kept in touch with the White House via the telephone installed at the Long Key dock. Mail pouches were flown into Miami, delivered by train to Long Key, and taken by courier to the president's secretary aboard the *Kilkenny*. The reporters and magazine writers stayed close to the dock so they could grill the courier to obtain scraps of news as soon as he came ashore to pick up mail and messages.[10]

On the second day out, the president landed a 45-pound sailfish after a half-hour fight. It was to be his largest catch of the trip. On the third day, while the *Saunterer* put into the Long Key dock to replenish food and water, Justice Stone's wife, Agnes, hauled in a 66-pound sailfish.[11]

By the sixth day at sea, Hoover had had enough. As *Time* magazine delicately put it, "The President's fishing had not been extraordinarily successful." In addition to the sailfish, he had caught a mackerel, four bonitos, and three barracuda. With Hoover having decided to end his vacation early and return to Washington, the *Saunterer* headed back to Long Key. During the evening of Saturday, February 15, the president went ashore and walked directly to his private railroad car, which was then attached to the northbound train. By early Monday morning he was back in Washington, tanned, somewhat rested, and perhaps a little disappointed.[12]

Agnes Stone's 66-pound sailfish was not only the largest fish taken during the presidential trip but also the largest sailfish taken by fishermen out of Long Key for the 1929–30 season, and her name was duly entered into the camp's record book. The Supreme Court justice's wife was awarded the prestigious Long Key Fishing Club gold pin, her catch barely exceeding the minimum of 65 pounds for the mid-sized sailfish category.

Although the president was a member of the club, his sailfish was 10 pounds below the minimum requirement for a silver pin, the lowest award. Determined to see that the president's catch received some form of recognition, the ever-tactful George Schutt asked for and received approval to have Hoover's fish prepared and mounted for hanging in the lounge of the Long Key Fishing Camp lodge. The *Catskill Recorder* reported: "His many Greene county friends will be interested to know that George is personally supervising the preparation of the President's big prize for proper display." And that is how Zane Grey's 125-pound sailfish caught in 1918 ended up sharing wall space with a 45-pound sailfish landed in 1930.[13]

During the season the manager oversaw a staff of about sixty employees. Most of them were quartered in dormitories on the bay side and were away from their homes and families from mid-December to mid-April. On February 6, 1920, a federal census enumerator listed fifty-nine people as working at the Long Key Fishing Camp. The following staffing chart of the camp is based on the federal occupation codes listed in the census.[14]

While he was manager of the Long Key Fishing Camp, L. P. Schutt recruited at least four people from the Catskills. T. B. "Brooks" Van Orden was brought in to manage the camp's fleet of boats in 1910. Phillip Warshaw of the Desmond Shore House in Leeds, New York, was hired in 1918 to be the camp's steward. Melvin Van Loa of Catskill was hired in 1920 to captain one of the camp's boats. The first "Catskillian" to be hired was probably John Scribner, Schutt's lifelong friend from Greene County. Reflecting the regard his boss had for him, Scribner was engaged as the caretaker of the camp.[15]

The caretaker was an important position at the seasonal resorts owned by the Florida East Coast Hotel Company. During the season, the manager was the senior, resident representative of the company; during the off-season, the caretaker held that position.

At the end of a season, the dining room, kitchen, lodge, and guest bungalows were closed and shuttered. The camp's boats were hauled up, serviced, and stored in the large boat sheds. The resort staff from the manager to the chambermaid left the island, many of them going to mountain or seaside resorts in the North, where they worked the summer and fall seasons.[16]

From late spring through most of fall, the caretaker and a helper were often the only Florida East Coast Hotel Company employees on the island. They were sometimes joined by maintenance men brought in to make repairs. The primary duties of the caretaker during this period were to maintain security and

Table 8.1. Long Key Fishing Camp staff positions

BUSINESS OFFICE	
Camp manager	1
Cashier	1
Secretary/clerk	1
HOTEL AND FOOD SERVICE	
Steward	1
Assistant steward	1
Head bellman	1
Bellman	4
Transportation manager	1
Maid	3
Chambermaid	1
Head waiter	1
Waiter	9
Waitress	1
Chef	1
Cook	3
LAUNDRY	
Manager	1
Laundry worker	4
MARINA	
Dockmaster	1
Dock hand	1
Bait house manager	1
BOATS AND LAUNCHES	
Manager/senior boatman	1
Boatman	4
Fisherman/guide	4
Machinist/mechanic	1
FACILITIES	
Caretaker	1
Foreman	1
Equipment operator	1
Carpenter	3
Painter	1
Laborer	3
Watchman	1
TOTAL STAFF	59

Source: U.S. Federal Census, enumerated in February 1920.

fire-watch, make minor repairs, prepare the facilities for bad weather including hurricanes, and to handle any other on-site issues that arose involving the camp.

Each December the full staff began to return, and preparations for opening the camp were commenced, including an intensive effort to clean the grounds and beach, activate the gas plant, and open and refresh the buildings. The boats were launched and the cabin cruisers and other watercraft made ready for use, the head chef restocked the pantry and ordered perishables, and the housekeeping staff saw to the preparation of rooms and cabins.

The caretaker position required a trustworthy, conscientious individual with good mechanical and construction skills, initiative, awareness of the need to keep costs in line, and ingenuity in using the equipment and materials at hand to fix facilities problems or to control them until help could arrive. In an emergency, he could call upon the Florida East Coast Railway maintenance crew located at the section camp about a half mile up the track.[17]

In late April 1910, the federal census enumerator listed Owen Moore as caretaker of the camp. It is believed that he was replaced shortly thereafter by John Scribner and that Scribner moved his wife, Ella, and their two sons from the Catskill Mountains to Long Key probably sometime around 1910. The boys grew into manhood on the island, leaving in 1918 to join the Navy.[18]

In addition to his caretaker duties, John served as the Long Key postmaster, freeing L. P. Schutt of that responsibility. Later Ella became the postmistress. In 1930, when John and Ella both turned sixty-nine, they decided to retire and move to Miami. The impending departure of John Scribner was not a trivial matter; it could have been very difficult to find a satisfactory replacement for him had the new postmistress not come forward.[19]

9

The Last Caretaker

The Conchs, of whom incidental mention has already been made, inhabit one portion of the island. Their quarter is called Conch town. They were originally Bahamans, who settled in Key West, and pursued wrecking for a livelihood. Whether a man is a native Bahaman, resident in Key West, or whether he is born in Key West, seems to make no difference: he is known as a Conch.

The name of Conch is taken from that of the large shell-fish which are found in great numbers in the waters of the Gulf.

—Richard Meade Bache,
The Young Wrecker of the Florida Reef

Cornelia Sawyer replaced Ella Scribner as the postmistress of the Long Key Post Office sometime in the late 1920s. She probably had the help of L. P. Schutt in obtaining the position; Cornelia needed the job, even if it was 60 miles from her home.

Cornelia Curry Roberts married Howard Reynold Jefferson Sawyer in 1906 at Key West; both were "Conchs." Howard was born in the Bahamas, where he resided until sometime after 1883, when his family moved to the Island City. Cornelia was born in Key West, but her ancestors had also migrated from the Bahamas.

By March 1922, Cornelia and her thirty-nine-year-old husband had a nice family of their own, a boy four months old and two girls ages six and fourteen. They lived comfortably in a large, two-story, wood-frame residence known as the "Bahama House" because it was originally constructed in the Bahamas. In 1847, the house was dismantled and shipped to Key West, where it was reassembled on what was then the eastern fringe of the town; as the town grew and the street system expanded around it, the house ended up on the southwest corner of the intersection of Williams and Eaton Streets.[1]

Howard Sawyer was elected tax assessor of Monroe County in 1922. According to the local newspaper, he was one of the most popular men in the county. His popularity went beyond the Florida Keys as was evidenced in Jacksonville while he was attending the Great Council of Florida of the Improved Order of Red Men of Florida.[2] The Society of Red Men evolved in 1813 from several secret patriotic societies. Inner discord and the practice of holding rowdy meetings in bars caused membership to dwindle until the group ceased to exist by 1830. The Improved Order of Red Men was formed in 1834 based on the original organization, but with changes to protect against the problems that had caused the predecessor organization to self-destruct.

The Improved Order of Red Men incorporated rituals and terminology from Native American tribes. This practice was carried to the point of referring to members' wives as "squaws" and money as "wampum." The tribal councils operated under the auspices of state councils and ultimately the national Grand Council of the United States. A special effort was made to overcome the undesirable reputation the predecessor organization had acquired

Howard Sawyer was thirty-six and had a promising political future when this photograph was taken in 1919. Courtesy of Patricia J. Duane.

by performing charitable activities and advocating patriotic ideals and goals that perpetuated the beliefs fundamental to the establishment of the United States. By the 1920s, the fraternity was said to have more than a half million members. Membership in the order, if not a prerequisite, was certainly desirable for men with political ambitions.[3]

The Key West tribal council had been a very active part of the order, and Howard Sawyer had made the most of his participation. Tuesday, March 21, 1922, was the culmination of many hours of service on his part. The Florida Council met in Jacksonville that day with the Great Grand Sachem, John Roberts of Key West, presiding. During the proceedings, Key West was selected as the site for the next annual meeting of the Florida Council, and Howard Sawyer was elected to the high office of Great Sachem Sagamore, which positioned him to become the Great Grand Sachem the next year. All in all it was a great day for Howard and the Key West delegation.[4]

That evening the delegates assembled for dinner, and Howard gave an acceptance speech described as "brilliant" by a Jacksonville newspaper. At quarter to midnight, he and a party of fellow delegates left the Red Men's hall for the short walk back to their hotel. As he was crossing a street, a speeding car careened around the corner and struck him. The *Florida Times-Union* reported what happened next:

> His body was knocked or dragged some distance. Several women and children—some of whom narrowly escaped death—screamed. However, the automobile—painted green with a brown top—did not stop. It sped away swiftly from the scene of the accident. . . . His body broken and shattered, and his head badly injured, Sawyer was rendered unconscious. He was picked up and carried to 119 Newnan street, but he gasped his last breath about 10 minutes after the death car dashed away.[5]

Howard's horrible death devastated Cornelia and her family. When the emotional shock subsided, she realized she was now the breadwinner for her family. Rather than feeling sorry for herself, Cornelia immediately applied to serve out the remainder of her husband's term of office, and by the end of the month, she was appointed Monroe County tax assessor by Governor Cary Hardee. When the term expired in December, Cornelia was recommissioned to serve for two more years.[6]

During her last year in office, tragedy struck again when her son contracted diphtheria. The diphtheria bacteria produce an extraordinarily potent toxin that can cause a tough, fiber-like membrane to grow on the tonsils and in the respiratory tract and block airways. The toxin is powerful enough to dissolve tissue and gain entry into the bloodstream, where it can spread to vital organs and paralyze muscles. As the disease progresses, the patient suffers extreme pain, and the damage can become so extensive that death may occur due to suffocation, heart failure, or a number of other causes.

An effective treatment was available in the 1920s, but the condition often was initially misdiagnosed as tonsillitis, and the resulting delay in the administration of lifesaving antitoxins frequently proved fatal. Even when it was diagnosed correctly, some physicians were hesitant to inject the dosages of antitoxin needed to be effective. Children between ages two and ten were most vulnerable to the disease.[7]

Howard Jefferson Sawyer Jr. was two years, one month, and thirteen days old when, after a few weeks of illness, he died on January 31, 1924. Because the disease is contagious, there was no funeral and his body was buried the same day.[8]

In less than two years, Cornelia had lost her husband and her only son. She carried the burden of those traumatic experiences into the fall elections as she sought to retain her position as tax assessor; however, on December 19, 1924, her opponent, Eugene L. Albury, assumed the office of Monroe County tax assessor and Cornelia became unemployed.[9]

She did what she could to provide for the basic needs of her two remaining children and rented out the upstairs rooms of the Bahama House. The family had the strong support of relatives and friends throughout the close-knit island community. During this difficult time, their church became the center for their fellowship and spiritual comfort.

The Sawyers attended the First Methodist (Old Stone) Church two blocks west of the Bahama House. Around 1925, Cornelia noticed that one of her daughters was taking special care to look her best when attending the Sunday service. It did not take her long to figure out why.

James Edwin Duane Jr. was a slim, sociable sailor from Pulaski, Virginia. He had enlisted in the Navy in 1915, the same year that Zane Grey's western novel *The Lone Star Ranger* became his first book to make the coveted best-seller list. The hero in the book was an outlaw named Buck Duane who became a legendary Texas Ranger. It was not long before James Duane was nicknamed "Buck" by his shipmates. The moniker stuck and was used thereafter by friends and family.

Buck's naval career began too late for him to see action in the Great War, and he ended up being stationed at Key West. He was in his mid-twenties when he heard that a lot of "good-looking ladies" went to the Old Stone Church. One Sunday he decided to investigate and came away a changed man.

In 1925, Lindy Sawyer (*left*) was a winsome Conch whose ancestors had moved to Key West from the Bahamas during the 1800s. She attracted the attention of James "Buck" Duane from Virginia (*right*), who had joined the Navy too late to see combat in the Great War and ended up being stationed in Key West as an ambulance driver. Courtesy of Patricia J. Duane.

It was not the beautiful stained-glass windows, the impressive stone sanctuary, or the vibrant ecclesiastical oratory that impressed him, but the winsome smile of eighteen-year-old Ethelind (Lindy) Louise Sawyer.

After the initial encounter, Buck was smitten and began to attend church regularly to flirt with Lindy. Aware that more than a casual attraction was developing between her eldest daughter and the sailor, Cornelia made it clear that she did not want Lindy marrying a man in the Navy. If this was intended to discourage Buck, it failed, and he began to express his love in an unusual way. His job was to drive the ambulance for the Marine Hospital, and each time he passed the Bahama House on trips for gas or other nonemergencies, he would sound the siren.

Soon the wail of the siren was occurring with annoying regularity. When the romantic significance of the shrieking became known, Cornelia's neighbors urged her to let Lindy marry the fellow and be done with it! Peace was restored when Buck was honorably discharged from the Navy and Cornelia gave her consent. The couple was married in June 1927 at the Old Stone Church, and the newlyweds headed north for their honeymoon and a visit with the groom's parents in Allentown, Pennsylvania.

Cornelia and her fourteen-year-old daughter, Lois, now made up the Sawyer household at the Bahama House. While renting the upstairs rooms helped, without a regular paycheck coming in, Cornelia still struggled financially; she was determined to find a job. At about this time it is believed that L. P. Schutt, who was managing the Casa Marina and was well-acquainted with the tax assessor's office, talked to his son George, and the post-office position at Long Key was made available to the widow. Although the job required her to be at Long Key during the week, she could return by train to Key West for the weekends. Since Lois was old enough to take care of herself, and there were relatives nearby to look in on her when her mother was away, Cornelia became the Long Key postmistress.

Meanwhile in Allentown, personable and outgoing Buck found work as an insurance salesman, and the newlyweds stayed on at his parent's home.

Cornelia Sawyer was the Long Key postmistress during the late 1920s and early 1930s. She was a pragmatic, resilient woman. Courtesy of Patricia J. Duane.

In 1928, their first child, Patricia, was born and they moved to New Jersey. A year later, the nation's economy collapsed and the Great Depression commenced; life insurance became one of the things many people felt they could do without to save money. With his income drying up, Buck began to look for other options, but unemployment was rampant. Even the steel plant his father managed was soon affected, and it became clear that going back to Allentown and staying with his parents was not an alternative. As the weeks passed, their situation became more desperate; then a call from his mother-in-law brought a glimmer of hope.

When Cornelia heard that John Scribner was retiring, she asked George Schutt if her son-in-law could be considered for the caretaker position at the Long Key Fishing Camp and received an encouraging response. With employment prospects in New Jersey not expected to improve anytime soon, Buck and Lindy moved back to the Bahama House with their daughter, and he applied for the position. By the fall of 1930 James Duane was the new caretaker of the fishing camp.

Buck settled into his job. When guests were at the camp, usually from January into April, the emphasis was on operating and maintaining the gas plant and water-distribution systems, emergency repairs in guest areas, keeping the grounds clean and the beach clear of seaweed and other tidal debris. During

This may have been an end-of-the-season group photograph of some of the camp staff, circa 1930. Buck Duane is second from the left; his mother-in-law, Cornelia Sawyer, is wearing the black hat. Courtesy of Patricia J. Duane.

Four-year-old Patricia Duane poses on her tricycle in 1932. An adventurous child, she has many fond memories of the Long Key Fishing Camp while her father was the caretaker there. Courtesy of Patricia J. Duane.

the off-season from May to November, he was busy making repairs, painting, and doing minor renovations. The off-season was an especially happy time for the family because Lindy and Pat stayed with him in the caretaker's cabin. Cornelia, as postmistress, had her own quarters when she was at the camp.

When George Schutt's dog had a litter of puppies in 1933, he allowed four-year-old Pat Duane to pick one for a pet. White with patches of black, the Springer spaniel was named "Mike" and became an important part of the Duane family. Mike stayed at Long Key throughout the year, assisting Buck with camp security.

While Lindy was near term with their second child, Buck temporarily assumed the duties of the Long Key postmaster in addition to being caretaker so that Cornelia could stay in Key West with Lindy. As summer of 1933 drew to a close, Lindy gave birth to their second daughter, Jacquelyn. All things considered, his employment at the fishing camp was working out well for Buck and his expanding family. Many other people in the Florida Keys were not as fortunate.[10]

10

The Depression and the Good Life at Long Key

One year ago today, the Florida Emergency Relief Administration, headed by Julius F. Stone, Jr., took over the administration of most of the activities which were formerly carried on by the City of Key West and the County of Monroe. Three days earlier the city council and the board of county commissioners, by resolutions, had declared that the two political bodies were in a destitute condition financially and unable to carry on without assistance.

Their resolutions were addressed to Governor Dave Sholtz and in them "all legal powers conferred upon the officers" of the two bodies were surrendered. Since a large portion of the city's population was on the relief rolls, Governor Sholtz passed the problem to Administrator Stone. The Legislature of 1935 validated the action of the two local political organizations.

—*Florida Keys Sun* (Key West), July 5, 1935

The economic impact of the Great Depression hit the Florida Keys hard. The Florida East Coast Railway declared bankruptcy in 1931 and went into receivership, but remained in operation. The following year, financial pressures forced the Florida East Coast Hotel Company to close the Alcazar in St. Augustine and the Casa Marina in Key West. L. P. Schutt returned to his home in Haines Falls, New York, took sick, and died on June 30, 1933, at the age of seventy.[1]

The economic situation in the Florida Keys was grim by 1934. At Key West, Monroe County's economic center, the $44 million military complex that had swarmed with activity during the Great War had been deactivated two years earlier and only a small staff remained to keep the Navy's communications facility operating. More than ten thousand of the Island City's thirteen thousand people were on relief that summer. Tax revenues declined until the county and city could no longer pay their employees and debts. On July 2, 1934, the citizens of Monroe County and the City of Key West petitioned the governor to have the State of Florida take over their municipal affairs, in effect declaring the city and county governments insolvent.[2]

One of the brighter spots in the economic gloom that engulfed the Florida Keys was the Long Key Fishing Camp. There was some decline in business, but enough of its clients were sufficiently wealthy that the Great Depression did not discourage them from enjoying the resort.

Fishing was superb during the 1934 season, with 102 sailfish, 96 amberjack, and 100 dolphin (now called mahimahi) being taken. One guest landed a 132-pound Allison tuna that was the second-largest ever to be landed in Florida waters. Lieutenant Colonel Gillett caught the season's largest tarpon, weighing 106 pounds, while a young lady set a camp record bringing aboard a 14-pound mangrove snapper.

Anticipating that the 1935 season would be the busiest in several years, manager George Schutt opened the fishing camp on Christmas Eve, a week earlier than usual. Before the New Year rang in, the Countess of Suffolk had arrived with her servants, and Benny Crowninshield was on his way.[3]

The Long Key Fishing Club had eighty-five members in 1935, including Zane Grey, Herbert Hoover, the Countess and Lieutenant Colonel Gillett, the Cardezas, and Benny Crowninshield. Some other notable members were:

- Gifford Pinchot, governor of Pennsylvania.
- Col. Edwin Chance, a Philadelphia chemical engineering consultant, who during the Great War adapted soft-drink bottling methodology for the filling of poisonous gas artillery shells at the Edgewood Arsenal.[4]
- Fred C. N. Parke, renowned taxidermist of Bangor, Maine, who, according to one newspaper reporter, "has done for fish what Carl Akely, the famous sculptor-taxidermist, has accomplished in mounting the elephants of East Africa. Parke has caught the colors of the giant gaipe fish, those elusive, shimmering rainbow tints which begin to flicker, fade and disappear within a few moments after they have been taken from the sea."[5]

- Edwin C. vom Hofe, whose father, Edward, manufactured some of the finest fishing reels in the world. In 1929, the company produced a saltwater reel named the Long Key designed specifically for capturing the elusive bonefish. The reel featured an adjustable automatic tension drag, sliding gear transmission, and rim control.[6]
- John C. Cosseboom, a Rhode Island insurance businessman whose hobby was fly-fishing. He became internationally known for the flies he invented, particularly those for salmon fishing.[7]

At the annual meeting of the Long Key Fishing Club in March 1935, outgoing president Henry Fisher, head of Standard Oil of New York, turned the gavel over to Jack Russell, outfitter and guide of national repute. In August 1935, the *New York Times* proclaimed the Long Key Fishing Club "one of the leading organizations of its kind in Florida, its membership roll including the names of prominent sportsmen from all over the country." The future of the Long Key resort seemed to be as bright as the sparkling waters around it.[8]

The summers of 1934 and 1935 were particularly happy times for the Duane family. Lindy and the children stayed with Buck through the summer. Although Buck had work to do, his schedule was flexible. With Mike tagging

The westernmost building on the ocean side of the camp was the Bonita, the caretaker's home. In this photograph, it is the building closest to the man walking on the path. The west side of the lodge and dining hall can be seen in the background. Courtesy of the Monroe County Public Library.

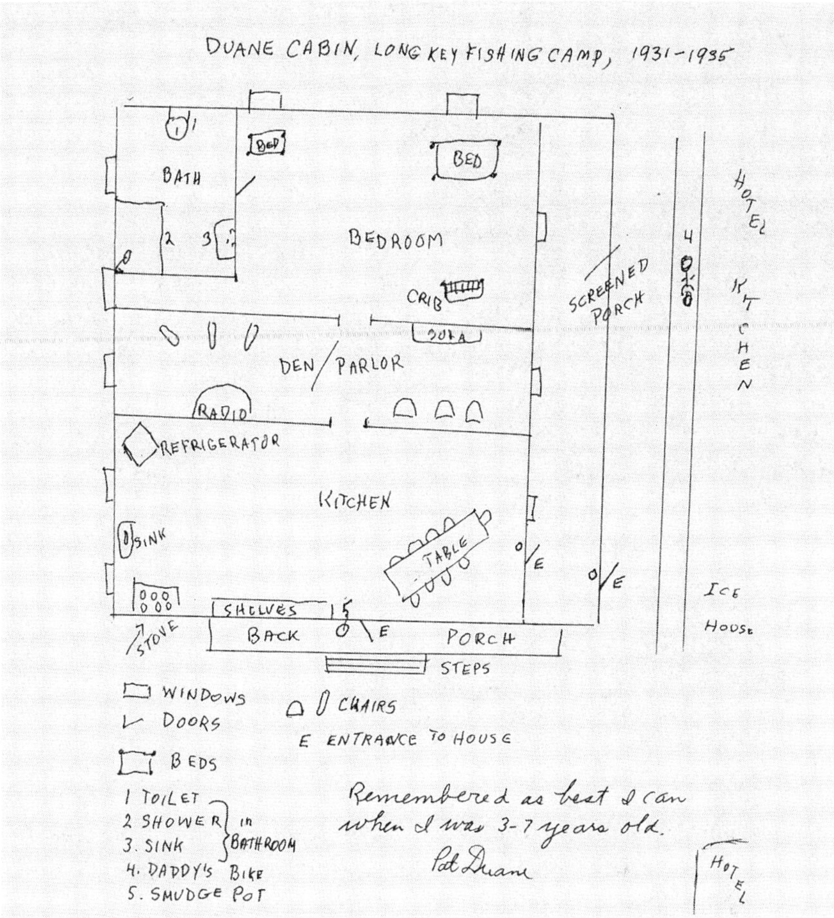

Pat Duane drew this sketch of the layout of the caretaker's bungalow seventy-five years after she lived there. The Bonita had an indoor bathroom with shower and a parlor with a broadcast-band radio. Smudge pots near the exterior doorways were kept burning during the day to discourage mosquitoes from entering the house. The refrigerator was actually an icebox; ice and potable water were delivered regularly by train, including during the off-season. Courtesy of Patricia J. Duane.

along, the family fished, swam, and went beachcombing, safe in their private world that seemed far, far away from the hard times brought on by the Great Depression.

One of Buck's chores involved entering the bungalows to empty drains and turn off the water. His daughter Pat enjoyed going with him as he made his rounds and looking at the furnishings inside the large homes reserved for the wealthy. There were superbly crafted statues, elegant furniture, hand-woven

Buck Duane used this bicycle to get around the camp. The small bike on the right was his daughter Pat's. This circa 1935 photograph was taken from the loading dock of the kitchen/icehouse and shows the screened porch of the caretaker's house. Courtesy of Patricia J. Duane.

carpets, and cabinets with windows displaying expensive china, but what fascinated her most was a bowl filled with large, transparent, blue-tinted marbles. Her father explained that the marbles were "puries" made of fine glass with no entrapped bubbles or other imperfections. She was not allowed to touch them, which made them all the more attractive.

The summer of 1935 was especially memorable for the Duanes' eldest daughter. Now almost seven, Pat often went about the camp unaccompanied. Buck had obtained a small bike for her, and she would ride the boardwalk all around the resort and then follow the path through the tunnel under the embankment ending up at the marina. The long, L-shaped dock became one of her favorite places. She played "chicken" with herself, riding as fast as she could toward the end that pointed toward the viaduct and then skidding to a stop, the challenge being to see how close she could come without going overboard.

On another occasion she went hiking, straying well beyond the east boundary of the resort's property before she realized she was surrounded by the ominous buzzing of rattlesnakes. Lost, she slowly moved away from the snakes,

Buck Duane was his own boss for most of the year. During the off-season, there was no need to shave regularly or to keep shirts buttoned. Courtesy of Patricia J. Duane.

The end of the doglegged dock at the marina pointed toward the Long Key Viaduct. Pat Duane used to play "chicken" on her bike during the summer, going full speed and then braking to see how close she could come to the end. This postcard scene is from around 1910. The ladies in the long dresses were probably comfortable since the breeze coming off Florida Bay could be quite chilly during the winter. Thomas Neil Knowles Collection.

found the railroad track, said a short prayer asking for help in choosing the right direction to follow the rails, and ended up back at the fishing camp. Despite her adventurous spirit, she escaped serious injury.

It would have been paradise except for the mosquitoes, which were voracious during the warmer off-season. As Pat recalled: "The mosquitoes were almost always bad. We kept smudge pots burning at all the entrances to the house so they wouldn't get in. After a while I became immune to their bite and wasn't bothered by them." One place free of the flying insects where there was almost always a cool breeze was the screened veranda on the first floor of the lodge. At the southwest corner, a regulation punching bag had been hung from the ceiling. Pat and her baby sister, Jacque, would play on the broad porch while their parents took turns working out with the big leather bag. Asked if her mother made a serious effort, Pat responded: "Yes, she really did! My father, however, was much better. I can see him putting the boxing gloves on her even now."

Cornelia Sawyer keeps an eye on her granddaughter Jaqueline Duane as she walks on the "little dock" in June 1935. Buck built the dock on the ocean side of the camp and cleaned the sea bottom at its end so that his family and guests could have a place to swim without having to wade out across the seaweed and rocks to reach sufficient depth. He installed a submerged chicken-wire fence around the area to discourage barracudas and other fish from disturbing the swimmers. Courtesy of Patricia J. Duane.

Waiting for the train to Key West, Cornelia Sawyer (in black hat) poses with her daughters Lois (*left*) and Lindy (*right*). The woman holding the black bag is believed to be the camp's bookkeeper. The tank on the tower in the background at the right supplied salt water to the camp, which was used for fire mains, the sanitary sewer system, and general washing. Freshwater stored in the cypress tanks behind Lois and the bookkeeper was a precious commodity. The path through the palm trees on the left leads to the marina. Courtesy of Patricia J. Duane.

Nighttime at Long Key during the off-season could be a magical time for a little girl. The amber glow of the kerosene lamps that provided lighting inside the caretaker's house gave it an aura of coziness. The gas lamps that gaily lit the grounds of the camp in the evenings during the season were inoperative because the acetylene gas plant was shut down after the guests left. On most nights, the stars and moon bathed the camp with their special light, at times so strong that the white sand appeared to glow. "I don't remember it being really dark at night," Pat Duane recalled. "We used to go down to the big dock to watch the tarpon. Their eyes lit up at night."

The darkness could have a sinister aspect as well. The swaying palm trees that provided welcome shade during the day at night became the haunt of animated shadows as the bright moon played through the dancing fronds. There was also real danger. The hard times brought on by the Depression made the furnishings of the lodge and the large cottages of the wealthy a temptation to thieves. The caretaker's daughter recalled an incident that made her aware of their vulnerability.

It was very quiet at Long Key at night. One time in the middle of the night my father heard an outboard motor. He followed the sound and saw a small boat pull up near where my grandmother's cottage was. He had his rifle with him and hollered at the two men before he shot. He must have hit one of them because there was a little blood on the sand the next morning. Needless to say I was a bit afraid when night came for a while after that.[9]

At the beginning of August 1935, Buck received a letter from Walter Bennett, the official in charge of the U.S. Weather Bureau at Jacksonville, where a hurricane center had been established the previous month. The letter officially appointed Duane a "cooperative observer." As such, Buck's duties were to take readings from instruments located in a cabinet near his cabin at least twice a day and more often if requested by the Miami Weather Bureau. He was to report the readings daily by telephone and at the end of each month send in a summary listing all observations made during the period. This he did

During the off-season, the first-floor veranda of the lodge served as a recreation room for the Duane family. The screens kept out the mosquitoes, and the ocean breeze made it a pleasant place to be in the evenings as well as the daytime. While the children played with their toys, both Buck and Lindy worked out on a punching bag that hung on the porch near the corner shown in this photograph. Courtesy of Patricia J. Duane.

In August 1935, on the morning she was to leave for Key West, Buck and Lindy Duane fished from the shore and caught some bonefish. Pregnant with their third child, she assumed a pose intended to minimize the visibility of her swollen waistline. Courtesy of Patricia J. Duane.

diligently, proudly signing his reports and correspondence, "J. E. Duane, Jr., Co-operative observer, U. S. Weather Bureau, Long Key, Monroe Co., Fla." Buck enjoyed being a weatherman.[10]

The Duanes made the most of the last week of August. Cornelia and Lindy's sister Lois came up to the camp, and the whole family enjoyed the beach and being together. All too soon it was time to leave for Key West. "It was the Friday of the Labor Day weekend of 1935 and I didn't want to leave," recalled Pat, "but I was beginning the second grade on Tuesday and had to get ready for school." At 10:00 a.m. on the eve of that fateful holiday weekend, Pat and her sister boarded the Havana Special with their mother, grandmother, and aunt.[11]

Buck stood on the platform and waved good-bye as the train pulled out of the station. The knowledge that the resort was doing well and his job was secure must have been comforting, especially now that Lindy was in the second trimester of her third pregnancy. He had a job with real responsibility in a beautiful setting doing work he enjoyed. Buck had every reason to believe life would only get better; however, the winds of change were not far off and were headed his way.

11

Hurricanes

The wind system of the hurricane is more or less circular. When it passes over a given locality, the winds do not begin abruptly, but increase gradually.

At the outer limits of the hurricane the winds are only moderate breezes though characteristically gusty and fitful. They increase in force as the center approaches, though the highest winds are not at the exact center but generally from 5 to 15 miles, and sometimes even farther, therefrom. Records indicate that these strongest winds often reach and, for 5 minutes or more, maintain velocities of 75 to 100 miles per hour, and occasionally even 125 to 150 miles per hour, with gusts of still greater velocities. . . .

At the center of a tropical cyclone there is an area known as the "eye of the storm," where there is little or no wind. In this central area the sky sometimes clears so that the sun is visible by day and stars by night. The temperature in some cases rises and the air becomes drier. . . . All around this relative calm is the encircling wall of hurricane winds, which produce a rumbling or roaring sound. The diameter of the relatively calm center is not the same in all storms and may be as little as 7 miles, or less, but is rarely more than 20. It averages about 14 miles.

When the calm center, or "eye," of the storm passes over a place, the calm is preceded by winds of great violence from one direction and is followed by winds nearly equally violent from the opposite direction.

—I. R. Tannehill, *The Hurricane*

With Lindy and the children gone, the caretaker's cottage at the Long Key Fishing Camp was unusually quiet, but Buck was soon concerned with news that a storm was brewing. That was nothing new at this time of year. Twelve days earlier, the first hurricane of the 1935 season had been tracked by the Weather Bureau. Originating several hundred miles east of the Bahamas, it moved to the north then curved toward Bermuda, presenting no threat to the United States.[1]

Since Buck had become the Long Key caretaker, the Weather Bureau had tracked fifty-six tropical disturbances. Of these, twenty-seven became hurricanes. The paths of most of them did not threaten Long Key, but hurricanes in 1932, 1933, and 1934 had headed in the general direction of the Upper Florida Keys. The 1932 storm came closest to the camp, making landfall 35 miles south of Miami. Barely a hurricane, it did modest damage on the mainland and insignificant damage in the Florida Keys.[2]

Buck learned of the second tropical disturbance of the 1935 hurricane season when he called the Miami Weather Bureau to report his 6:00 p.m. observations. Later that evening, radio station WIOD in Miami broadcast a statement issued by the Weather Bureau's hurricane center at Jacksonville: "Conditions remain unsettled and slightly squally east of the Bahamas and north of Turks Island with evidence of a weak circulation but no strong winds. Seems to be working north-northwest or northward." The location given was more than 500 miles east of the Long Key Fishing Camp, and the northerly heading suggested that this could be another storm that would wander off into the Atlantic, but as the people who built the railroad down the Keys had learned, hurricanes could be unpredictable and ruthless.[3]

During the twelve years the Key West Extension was under construction, fewer than two hundred workers are estimated to have been killed on the job. This is a truly remarkable safety record in view of the fact that at peak activity several thousand workers were deployed on the Florida Keys, with many of them performing or exposed to dangerous tasks such as blasting with dynamite and working in cofferdams below sea level. Half of the Key West Extension fatalities were people in the Long Key area who worked on the viaduct and died during the October 1906 "Quarter Boat Hurricane."[4]

At 1:00 p.m. on the last day of August 1935, the Saturday before Labor Day, the hurricane center at Jacksonville issued its first storm advisory for the system of unsettled weather it had reported the previous evening. The first people in the Florida Keys to learn of its contents were the few who had access to broadcast-band radios and telephones; listening in on the telephone conversations of others was a common way to find out the latest local news. The advisory read: "Tropical disturbance of small diameter but considerable intensity central about 60 miles east of Long Island, Bahamas, apparently moving west northwestward, attended by strong shifting winds and probably gales near center. Caution advised southeastern Bahamas and ships in that vicinity. Further advises at 4 p.m." The weathermen now believed the strongest winds ranged from 39 mph to 63 mph and that the storm was intensifying and moving more toward the west.[5]

The Jacksonville office issued the advisory because in July 1935 the Weather Bureau had been directed by an act of Congress to decentralize and reorganize its hurricane service. The result was the establishment of hurricane centers at New Orleans, Jacksonville, Washington, D.C., and San Juan, Puerto Rico. Each center was responsible for monitoring a prescribed geographic zone, for tracking any tropical storms or hurricanes within its zone, and for the issuance of related warnings and advisories on behalf of the Weather Bureau for as long as the disturbance remained within its zone. The Jacksonville center's zone covered the Florida peninsula and extended to the south and east, including the area east of the Bahamas where the current tropical disturbance originated.[6]

Additional advisories issued at 4:00 p.m. and 9:30 p.m. indicated that the stormy weather was still moving west-northwestward, a heading that if sustained posed no threat to the Florida Keys. Overnight the situation changed; the fourth advisory issued at 9:30 Sunday morning indicated the storm was strengthening into a hurricane and was headed due west toward the Florida Straits between Havana and Key West. If it continued on this path, the worst part of the hurricane would pass over Key West. Now the safety of his family became Buck's concern.

There was some comfort in knowing his wife and mother-in-law, having been born and raised in Key West, knew how to prepare for and ride out a hurricane. Their home, the Bahama House, had weathered hurricanes in the Bahamas and Key West for more than ninety years. Although a bit run-down cosmetically, it remained structurally sound. One special concern this year was Lindy's condition; she did not need the added stress of enduring a hurricane while pregnant. At least she was in her hometown, and relatives and friends would come to her aid should she need help.[7]

The next advisory issued on Sunday afternoon read: "Advisory, 4 p.m.—Tropical disturbance central about 275 miles east of Havana, moving very slowly west or west-southwestward, probably accompanied by winds of

Cornelia Sawyer's home in Key West is known as the Bahama House. Originally constructed at Green Turtle Cay in the Bahamas, the house was dismantled and moved to Key West in 1847. Although it appears somewhat run-down in this 1930s photograph, it was structurally strong. The house continues to occupy the southwest corner of the intersection of Williams and Eaton Streets in Key West. Courtesy of Patricia J. Duane.

hurricane force over small area near center." The storm's heading was shifting more toward Havana and somewhat away from the Florida Keys. Buck knew this was no assurance that the Keys were out of danger.

The predicted storm track fostered grave concerns among the people in Key West who had endured the September 1919 hurricane. That storm's center had passed about 35 miles south of the Island City at midnight, heading west-northwest toward the Dry Tortugas and the Gulf of Mexico. Harry Boyer, who had been in charge of the Key West Weather Bureau, stated in his official report: "The storm that passed over Key West on September 9 and 10 was, without question, the most violent experienced since records at this station began. . . . In the terrific gusts that prevailed during the height of the storm, stanch brick structures had walls blown out and large vessels that had been firmly secured, were torn from their fastenings or moorings and blown on the banks." Boyer noted that almost all structures on the island were damaged with an estimated property loss of $2 million. Only three lives were lost at Key West, the Weather Bureau's warning of the hurricane's approach being credited with keeping the death toll so low. Key West had not experienced another devastating storm in the intervening sixteen years.[8]

After the City of Key West declared itself insolvent in July 1934 and its management was taken over by the state, administrators appointed by the governor worked with the Federal Emergency Relief Administration and the Works Project Administration to lead the city back toward financial stability. The rehabilitation plan was to make Key West a tourist destination similar to Bermuda. By the end of the summer of 1935, some progress had been made in removing the trash heaps that had accumulated on the streets due to lack of refuse service and in demolishing abandoned buildings. The current administrator, M. E. Gilfond, was not about to let a hurricane erase the gains made; faced with an increasing likelihood of the storm striking the city, he mobilized his forces to make preparations.[9]

The *Miami Herald* reported: "Emergency crews labored through Sunday placing storm shutters in position for quick boarding of windows and doors. Boats, rolling stock, and cabanas on the beaches were lashed down. Light dredges at work in the harbor were hastily towed to shore." The rehabilitation program had already torn down 145 dilapidated buildings, eliminating a source of deadly windborne debris. In addition, hundreds of buildings had been repaired and renovated, enhancing their stability and safety. "I think we're ready for any trouble," Gilfond said to a reporter for the *Miami Herald*. He told the *New York Times*, "Key West is boarded up so tight you can't recognize it."[10]

As if to validate Gilfond's actions, at 9:30 Sunday night the Weather Bureau ordered the display of northeast storm warnings. Weather stations and lighthouses from south of Miami, throughout the Florida Keys, and around the west coast to Fort Myers immediately displayed two red lanterns, one above the other. As soon as it was daylight, a red pennant above a square red flag with a black square at its center was hoisted. This configuration of lanterns and pennant/flag convey the ominous message that a storm of marked violence with winds beginning from the northeast may make landfall or pass close to the area. According to the Weather Bureau, the storm was 260 miles east of Havana and moving slowly westward, a course that if maintained would bring the center of the storm fewer than ninety miles from Key West; a slight change in its course would bring the most destructive part of the hurricane over the town.[11]

The Bahama House was equipped with storm shutters and could be made ready for a hurricane in less than an hour. Although Buck was not there to help Cornelia, her nineteen-year-old daughter Lois, and Lindy with the preparations, a man and his wife in their thirties were renting the second floor, and they lent a hand. Once the shutters were latched shut and the loose items in the yard and chairs on the porch were secured, the durable Bahama House was ready to weather another storm.[12]

A few blocks away, the downtown area buzzed with activity, not because of the storm warnings, but from the trainloads of people who had taken advantage of a special holiday excursion fare offered by the railroad. The Labor Day weekend was filled with festive events, and everyone seemed intent on making the most of their visit. Even though the Weather Bureau warned that a storm of marked violence was headed for the narrow throat of the Florida Straits between Havana and Key West, relatively few people left Sunday evening on the Miami-bound train. No one knew that would be the last train to the mainland.[13]

12

The Labor Day Hurricane

Our lives were so changed in just a matter of hours!

—Elizabeth Williams Chance,
a survivor of the 1935 Labor Day hurricane

September 2, 1935, Labor Day, began with a beautiful sunrise over a calm sea. Since it was the off-season, the Long Key Fishing Camp remained closed, and the beach and the grounds were deserted. The serenity stayed undisturbed until midmorning, when the train from Miami rumbled into the station. No. 75 made a brief stop to allow the new section foreman, his wife, and four children to disembark and for their baggage to be unloaded, then resumed its journey to Key West. Their arrival brought the total population of Long Key that fateful day to twenty: thirteen men, three women, and four children.[1]

The fishing camp had been closed since April and was not scheduled to welcome guests until late December. The guest cottages, lodge, and most of its other buildings had been shuttered and the boats hauled up and stored in the boat sheds when the season ended. The caretaker and several men who were at the camp making repairs kept busy securing loose materials and removing debris just in case the winds picked up.

Because of the activity in the tropics, the Miami Weather Bureau requested more frequent weather observations, which Buck was glad to provide. He kept up with the status of the storm by monitoring the radio in his cabin and chatting with the weathermen when he telephoned in his reports. The readings at Long Key through Sunday night and that morning were normal and gave no indication of the hurricane approaching Long Key. That was the conclusion

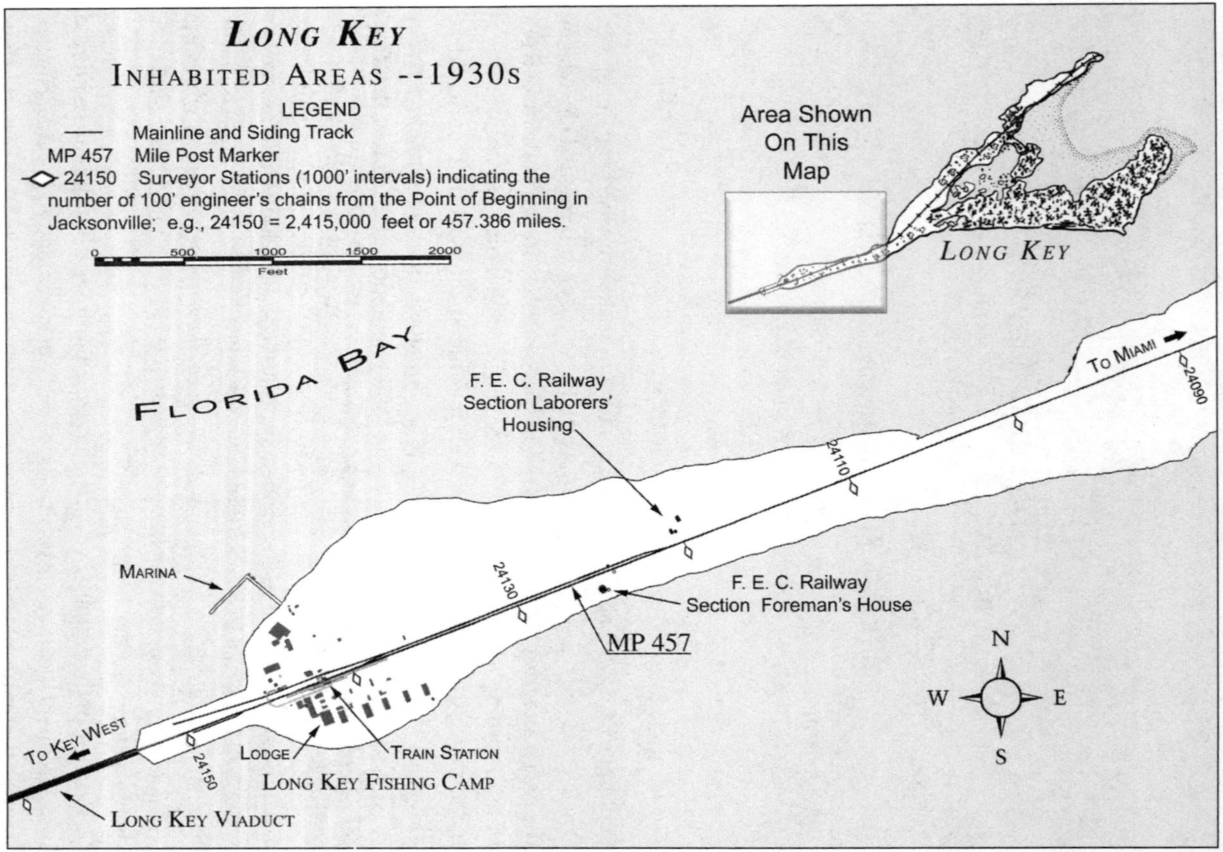

Long Key, showing the inhabited areas of the island in 1935. Map by Thomas Neil Knowles.

reached by the meteorologists at Jacksonville, whose 9:30 a.m. advisory stated that the storm was 200 miles east of Havana and moving slowly west toward the Florida Straits south of Key West.[2]

In addition to checking the barometer regularly, Buck watched the water for any unusual changes. Around 1:00 p.m., he noticed "a very slight swell" on the ocean side of the camp.[3]

At 1:30 p.m. the Jacksonville center issued another advisory that reported the storm's center 188 miles east of Havana with movement continuing slowly to the west.

Buck knew something was wrong when he made his observations at 2:00 p.m. The barometer was beginning to fall, and the water on the ocean side of the fishing camp heaved with growing swells. Heavy rain intermittently moved across the island driven by wind blowing from the bay at 25–30 mph. By 3:00 p.m. the swells had changed to large waves from the southeast that fought the wind as they crashed onto the sandy beach near the lodge and cottages. The barometer continued to fall, and by 4:00 p.m. was dropping at the alarming rate of .01 inch every five minutes. The north wind blew with such force that the rain stung any exposed parts of the body. Buck called the Miami Weather Bureau and reported the worsening conditions.[4]

He learned that another advisory was being issued by the Jacksonville center at 4:30 p.m. indicating the storm had made a radical change in direction, almost 90 degrees, and was now headed north toward the Florida Keys. He later told a reporter: "The storm approached Long Key about 4 p.m., Monday, when the increasing winds reached hurricane force. At that time the barometer was falling rapidly. With other employees of the camp consisting of a white man, three Negro men and a Negro woman, we barricaded ourselves in the caretaker's home."[5]

The caretaker's cabin was somewhat sheltered from the wind coming off the bay by the railroad embankment. Buck and his dog, Mike, along with carpenter Fran Thorn, labor foreman John Lockhart, the woman (believed to be Lockhart's common-law wife), and two laborers settled in to wait out the storm. Periodically Buck dashed out to the weather instruments cabinet to take readings. Although it was a short distance, flying sand and debris made each successive trip more hazardous as the storm intensified.[6]

At 6:00 p.m., Buck ran through the stinging rain and read the instruments. Convinced it would be too dangerous to make further trips, he removed the barometer and fought his way back to the cottage. The barometer was at 28.04 inches and still falling. Obviously the storm was headed their way.

The seas were now pounding the south shore. He ran over to the train

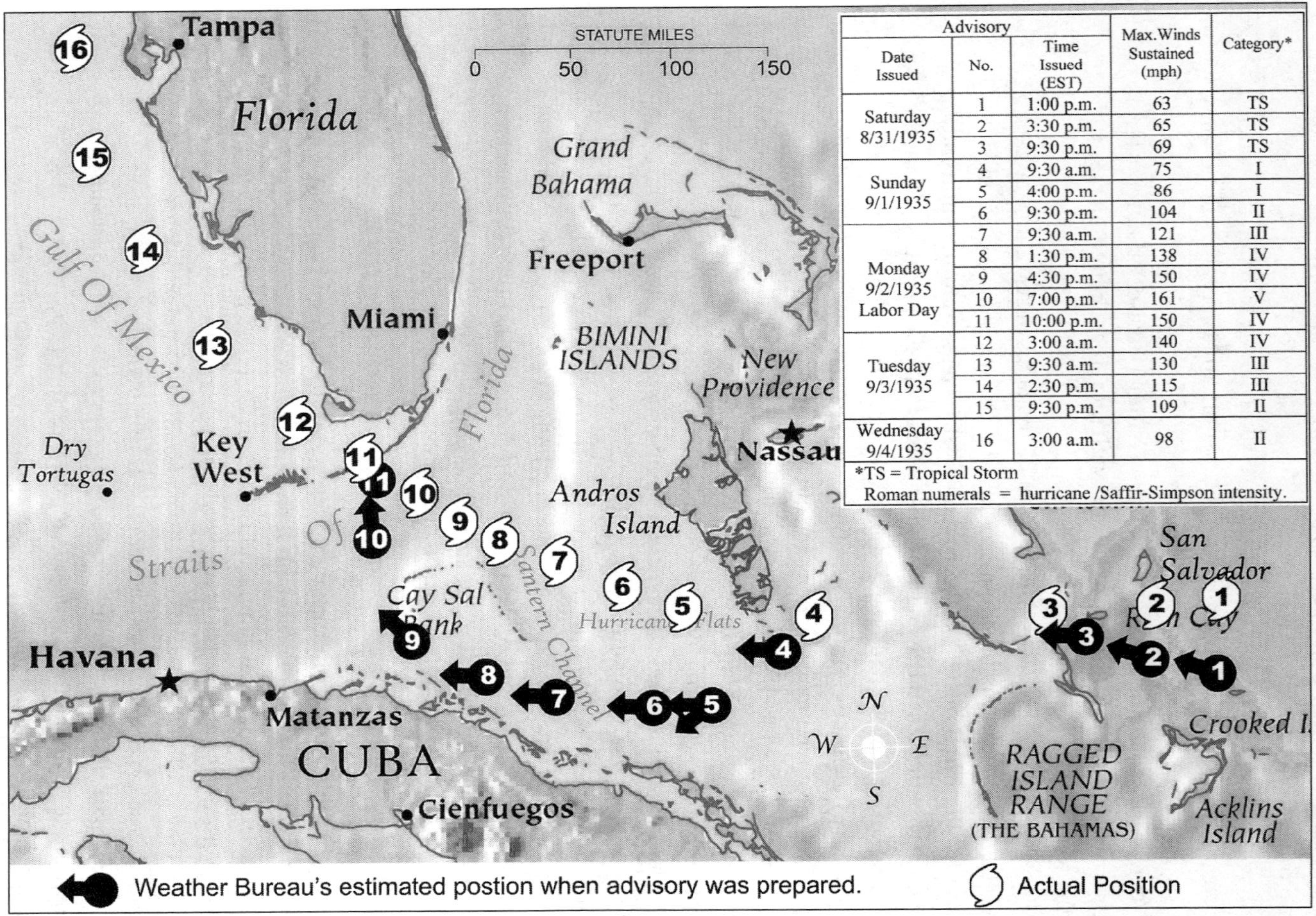

Advisory			Max. Winds Sustained (mph)	Category*
Date Issued	No.	Time Issued (EST)		
Saturday 8/31/1935	1	1:00 p.m.	63	TS
	2	3:30 p.m.	65	TS
	3	9:30 p.m.	69	TS
Sunday 9/1/1935	4	9:30 a.m.	75	I
	5	4:00 p.m.	86	I
	6	9:30 p.m.	104	II
Monday 9/2/1935 Labor Day	7	9:30 a.m.	121	III
	8	1:30 p.m.	138	IV
	9	4:30 p.m.	150	IV
	10	7:00 p.m.	161	V
	11	10:00 p.m.	150	IV
Tuesday 9/3/1935	12	3:00 a.m.	140	IV
	13	9:30 a.m.	130	III
	14	2:30 p.m.	115	III
	15	9:30 p.m.	109	II
Wednesday 9/4/1935	16	3:00 a.m.	98	II

*TS = Tropical Storm
Roman numerals = hurricane /Saffir-Simpson intensity.

Storm track of the 1935 Labor Day Hurricane, showing where the Weather Bureau believed the storm was located when various advisories were issued and the actual positions as determined after the event. Data Source: National Weather Service archives and the *Florida Hurricane Disaster*. Map by Thomas Neil Knowles.

station and tried to call the Miami Weather Bureau to make his report, but the line was dead. As he left the stationmaster's office, he could see that water covered the ground on the bay side and was creeping up the embankment. For the present, the raised roadbed was acting as a dam, keeping the wind-driven water from sweeping over the ocean side. He returned to the cottage with haste; it was no longer safe to venture outside.

At 6:45 p.m., Buck had just picked up the barometer and noted that the pressure was still falling when the cottage exploded. An 18-foot beam with an 8-inch by 8-inch cross-section had been wrenched by the wind from one of the large boat-storage sheds on the bay side and flung the distance of a football field, making a direct hit on the house. Amazingly, all of the occupants were unharmed, and the barometer Buck clutched in his hands was undamaged.

The caretaker's cottage was destroyed and no longer provided shelter from the wind and rain. The six people and dog made their way through the camp's kitchen and dining room to the two-story lodge. Safely inside the first-floor lounge by 7:00 p.m., they were soon joined by two other residents of the island, who reported water was flowing over the embankment. The needle on Buck's barometer continued to drop.

The air in the lounge was filled with the mist of atomized rain driven through cracks by the incessant wind. The noise level varied from painful to unbearable as blasts of air came in surges that lasted ten minutes before easing off a bit only to resume a few minutes later. During each of these intervals, the lodge was filled with the ungodly shrieking of the wind that combined with the fusillade of rocks, coconuts, timbers, and other debris to produce the frightful sound of a wild mob trying to force its way in. The sturdy lodge with its large piers driven into the bedrock shook with each assault.

The barrage continued unabated until 9:00 p.m. It was then Buck noticed the barometric pressure was falling very rapidly. Twenty minutes later, with the instrument indicating 27.22 inches, the lowest reading yet observed, the wind subsided until other noises from outside could be heard. He deduced they were in the eye of the hurricane. He knew that the lull was only temporary and that when the storm resumed in all its fury the wind would swing around and come from the ocean, sweeping across the open beach where there was nothing to shield the lodge. He also knew there was little chance that the weakened building could remain standing in such an exposed situation.

Hearing voices, the caretaker and his group left the lodge and found other people coming out of places of refuge, dazed and seeking guidance as to what to do. What happened next is best described by Duane in a report he prepared for the Weather Bureau after the storm:

> We now head for the last and only cottage that I think can or will stand the blow due to arrive shortly. A section hand reports that a white man, his wife and four children are in an unsafe place a half mile down the track. Aid is given them and now all hands, 20 in number, are in this cottage waiting patiently for what is to come.
>
> During this lull the sky is clear to northward—stars shining brightly and a very light breeze continued throughout the lull—no flat calm. About middle of lull (which lasted a timed 55 minutes) the sea began to lift up it seemed and rise very fast, this from ocean side of camp. I put my flashlight out on sea and could see walls of water which seemed many feet high.
>
> I had to race fast to regain the entrance of cottage, but water caught me waist deep. An idea as to the rapidity with which we were inundated may be gained when it is known that the writer was about 60 feet from the doorway of cottage. By the time I had gained the entrance the water was waist deep as just described. All people inside house now; water is lifting cottage from foundations. Cottage now floating.[7]

The cottage Buck thought would best withstand the storm was the Wahoo, recently built for the Countess of Suffolk. The sixteen adults, four children, and the caretaker's dog huddled in the darkness waiting for the onslaught to resume. The cabinets filled with fine china, the works of art hanging on the wall, and the expensive furniture that surrounded them were visible only during the brief intervals when a flashlight was turned on. Outside the sea was rising, flooding over the beach and then pouring into the house. The children were put on a large table, but the water level quickly reached the top and some of the men had to hold them to keep their heads above the water. The water continued to rise, making the situation more desperate by the minute. Suddenly the house lurched as it broke free of its foundation. The water level inside fell as the wood-frame structure began to float on the surface.[8]

The trailing wall of the hurricane's eye moved over the fishing camp at 10:15 p.m., and the high winds returned suddenly, drowning out any other sounds. Buck later recalled: "This was our first blast from S.S.W. which came full force. Seemed blast took one section of house away. House now breaking up—wind seemed stronger now than any time during storm."[9]

A flashlight pointed outside a window revealed the wrecked cottage was being washed out of the palm grove toward the sea. Buck, the carpenter, and one of the laborers jumped into the water to try to anchor the floating house, but the wind was too powerful and pushed the house away from them. Buck became separated from the other two men. He felt the nudge of a palm frond and clung desperately to it to keep from being swept away. He could see the beam of a flashlight frantically probing the darkness from one of the cottage's windows. The last thing he remembered before being knocked unconscious was the bobbing light growing smaller and smaller.[10]

In Key West, the biggest inconvenience weather-wise on Labor Day was an occasional squall. Although a few events were canceled, the movie theaters maintained their schedules and the bars and restaurants remained open for business. The usual stunning sunset was obscured by dark clouds that had been building all day. The bars took advantage of the décor afforded by their shuttered windows and put up handmade signs inviting all comers to hurricane parties. Later that night, occasional gusts of wind seemed to hold the promise of excitement, but tourists who had looked forward to experiencing their first hurricane were disappointed by the mildness of the storm. It is doubtful that many of the inebriated revelers were even awake at 2:56 Tuesday morning when the maximum wind of 46 mph was recorded at the weather station at the west end of Eaton Street.[11]

The 12,000-plus people in Key West had no inkling of the devastation and carnage taking place on the Upper Keys. The telephone/telegraph lines that were strung along the railroad right-of-way on poles and over the water on brackets attached to the bridges were vulnerable to even moderate storms so it was not alarming when those communications were disrupted beyond Marathon early Labor Day evening. Concern began to mount when the telegraph and telephone lines that ran due north from Key West via submerged cable to Punta Rassa on the mainland's west coast stopped working at 3:30 a.m.[12]

At the Bahama House, seven-year-old Pat Duane finally slept soundly after having overcome the anticipation of beginning another school year in the morning. Her mother did not seem worried about the storm; Lindy may have had concerns about Buck, but if she did, she concealed them from her children. It was just as well she was unaware of what her husband was enduring.[13]

13

The Long Road Home

> Asked how the twenty inhabitants of Long Key had spent the long night of terror, what they talked about and what they did, Mr. Duane said that the entire night was spent by all in the party in earnest, sincere prayer. Several times the members of the party bade each other goodbye, thinking their next moment would be their last.
>
> "At a time like that," said Mr. Duane, "there does not seem to be much to talk about. We thought our time had come and what we most desired was to get ourselves in shape to face our God."
>
> —*Florida Keys Sun* (Key West), September 6, 1935

At 2:25 a.m. Tuesday, Buck opened his eyes and looked at his watch, which was still working. He had been unconscious for four hours. Then he realized he was lodged in the top of a coconut tree 20 feet above the ground. All the water had receded from the island. The cottage that had carried his companions out to sea was now back on shore. "I dropped from the tree and regained the cottage after great difficulty where I found all people safe. A barometer found in the cottage was showing signs of going up but very, very slowly," he later wrote. The two men who had jumped into the water with Buck were missing.[1]

The worst of the storm was past, but the howls of hurricane winds accompanied by "terrific lightning flashes" continued until 5:00 a.m. Strong winds and stinging rain kept the group in what was left of the cottage for most of the morning. Later the two missing men were found unharmed, pinned under a pile of debris that had washed up onto the railroad embankment.[2]

By afternoon the weather had moderated enough so that they could scavenge for canned goods and bottled drinks. The destruction of the fishing camp was complete; anything that had survived the wind was destroyed by the rushing water. Fortunately, no one on the island had been killed, and injuries were limited to minor cuts and scratches. They could survive for a while on salvaged canned goods and by collecting rainwater from occasional squalls, but not for long. The worst part of the situation was the lack of contact with the outside world and the fear that no one knew of their plight.

There was no means by which the group could leave the island on their own. The boat-storage buildings and all vessels within had been wrecked. If a working handcar could be found, it would do no good; there was no useable track to put it on. There were places within hiking distance that had telegraph/telephone facilities. Craig is only 5 miles to the east, and the ferry terminal on Lower Matecumbe Key 2 miles beyond that, but going east would be problematic. The direction of the hurricane's winds just before and after the calm indicate that the most powerful part of the storm passed north of the fishing camp going from east to west. This meant that Craig and probably the islands above were at least as badly damaged as Long Key, probably worse. The railroad track coming from that direction was twisted off its roadbed, suggesting that the damage up the line was horrific; it was possible that the fills and viaduct to Craig had been washed out. Even if one could get there, the lines to the mainland would probably not be working.

Going west across the Long Key Viaduct appeared to offer the best chance for getting help. A railroad section gang station was at Grassy Key 7 miles away, and the settlement of Marathon 10 miles beyond that. A walk up the approach to the viaduct revealed that all of the railroad track had been removed from the roadbed and probably was in the water on the ocean side. Standing on the abutment where the viaduct begins, Buck could see the ragged end of the track 50 feet away dangling above the water. Although the track was gone from the viaduct, the structure appeared to be intact and much of the roadbed fill remained in place. What lay beyond was unknown, but Buck decided it was worth a try.[3]

Early the next morning, he bid farewell to the other survivors and left the camp with his dog. Stripped of the rails and ties, the viaduct looked strange, like a white, heavenly sidewalk stretching toward the sky. After walking a mile and a half, he reached the highest part, 30 feet above the water and could see that the viaduct was intact all the way to its west end, but not a foot of track remained on the roadbed.

At the west end of the viaduct, the railroad track reappeared on the ocean side 35 feet from its roadbed. The west approach was a gentle slope dropping 20 feet over 4 miles to the section gang station. Three fills connected by two small viaducts carried the trains from the Long Key viaduct to the east end of Grassy Key.

Over the next quarter mile, the twisted metal rails gradually returned to the roadbed. The going was rough for both man and dog, especially where the track was pushed aside and the roadbed was eroded. The track remained on the centerline for about a mile, but it was covered with rocks and piles of seaweed, requiring them to pick their way over the path of least resistance. At the first of the small viaducts, Tom's Harbor Viaduct No. 3, the track disappeared again.

Originally built as wooden trestles, the bridges across Tom's Harbor had been replaced with concrete viaducts in 1916. The two structures withstood the onslaught of the storm, but the track had been wrenched from their roadbeds and pushed into the water on the ocean side. At the west end of the second viaduct, the track returned to its intended centerline.

The weather was a mix of squalls followed by bursts of sunshine shooting through openings in the scudding clouds. The squalls sometimes contained gusts of wind strong enough to push Buck off balance, a particularly dangerous situation when he was crossing the narrow viaducts. At the east end of Grassy Key, he found more evidence of massive flows of water and powerful wind, the track having been pushed 50 feet toward the ocean side and the roadbed severely eroded. A little farther down, what was left of the highway leading to the Grassy Key ferry landing came into view on the bay side.

When the highway between the mainland and Key West was completed in January 1928, there was a 36-mile water gap between No Name Key and Lower Matecumbe Key that was covered by ferries. The ferries were slow, typically taking four-and-a-half hours to make the trip one way if there were no problems. To reduce overall travel time and give vehicular access to more islands, a paved road with ferry landings at each end was built from Grassy Key to Hog Key just west of Marathon. For most of its 13 miles, the highway ran adjacent to the railroad mainline passing over seven islands in the middle of the original water gap. No bridges had to be built for the Grassy Key–Hog Key highway since the islands were already connected by railroad fills that accommodated the roadway. When completed in the fall of 1928, the ferry routes were changed; one ferry covered the 14-mile gap between east end of

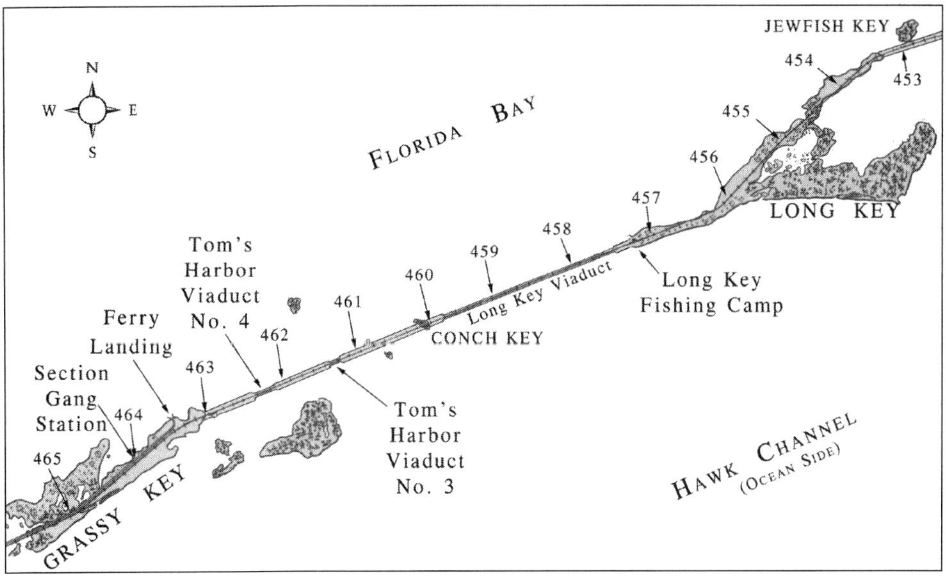

Long Key to Grassy Key, the first leg of Duane's hike. Map by Thomas Neil Knowles.

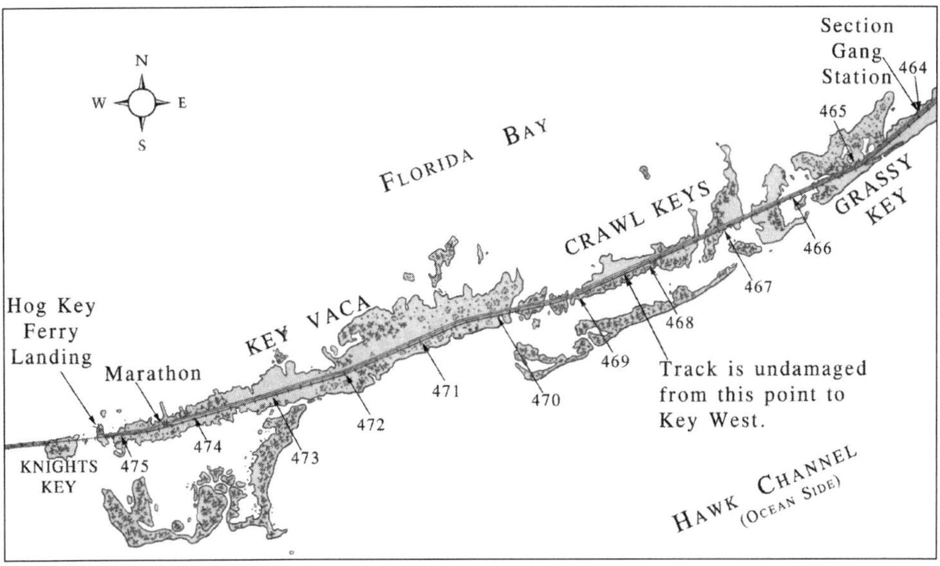

Grassy Key to Key Vaca, the second leg of Duane's hike. Map by Thomas Neil Knowles.

Grassy Key and the west end of Lower Matecumbe, while another ferry plied the 12 miles between Hog Key and No Name Key. The total time vehicles had to spend on ferries was cut almost in half.[4]

As Buck approached the eastern end of the highway, he could see it was severely eroded. This did not bode well for the section gang station located about three-quarters of a mile farther west.

The Florida East Coast Railway constructed facilities for maintenance crews and their equipment at intervals along the Key West Extension. A typical section gang camp consisted of a foreman's house, laborers' quarters, a tool shed, material storage area, and water tanks. The Grassy Key facility was located on the bay side of the track just west of milepost 464.[5]

It was eerily quiet as Buck approached the place; no insect noise, no birds, no human sounds—just an occasional rustle of debris when a gust of wind whisked over the torn landscape. The twisted mainline track lay 25 feet from its roadbed on the ocean side. A few badly eroded patches of roadbed were the only suggestion that a half-mile-long siding had run between the mainline and the compound. The four buildings that had housed the laborers were gone. The foreman's house was still standing although severely damaged. There were no bodies to be seen and no clues of what had happened to the inhabitants. Later he would learn that the foreman, his family, and most of the section hands had evacuated to Marathon and survived, but two men and the wife and child of one of them had chosen not to leave and were swept away and drowned.[6]

Tired and bruised from scrambling over debris and gouged fill, Buck and Mike trudged on; the railroad station at Marathon was still 10 miles away. For the next mile, the mainline track lay mangled on the ocean side of the roadbed. A little beyond the middle of the island, at milepost 465, the track was gone; it reappeared a half mile farther down. For the next 3 miles, it meandered over the fills and islands of the Crawl Keys, going off-center toward the ocean and back again several times. At the west end of the Crawl Keys, about 6 miles east of the Marathon station, the track came back onto the centerline of the roadbed and stayed there. Beyond that point, it appeared to be sound with no visible damage to the rails or bed.[7]

Buck and Mike still had to make their way around the debris that littered the mainline and the highway as they crossed onto Key Vaca, but the going was much easier and got better the farther they went. Finally, buildings and people came into view; they had arrived at Marathon.

The origin of the settlement's name is not clear. Some say that a civil engineer named it after Marathon, New York, which is near Cornell University where some of the Florida East Coast Railway technical staff received their education. Another theory is that the moniker was a derisive nickname supplied by construction workers who were under great pressure to transform the west end of Key Vaca and the surrounding area (Knights Key, Hog Key, and Boot Key) from a wilderness into a sprawling supply depot and equipment-repair center for the Florida East Coast Railway.[8]

From a humble tent encampment in 1906 sprang a complex switchyard, heavy-equipment-repair shops, marine railways, warehouses, tank farms, a hotel, employee housing, a school, and recreational and commissary facilities that transformed quiet bays and mangrove-shrouded islands into a thriving industrial complex. By 1910, Marathon was a community with families living in a residential area and a school with twelve children enrolled.

Two years later, Henry Flagler rode the first train from Miami to Key West, officially declaring the line operational. The railroad company began reducing the construction workforce on the Florida Keys. The school in Marathon had to be closed in 1913 due to lack of students. By 1918 the population had reverted to near preconstruction levels. In the spring of 1935, when the State of Florida census was taken, only 142 people were listed as living in the Marathon area. Deserted railway buildings stood in various states of decay, and worn-out machinery, barges, and other abandoned equipment sat ashore and in the shallows, rusting away.[9]

To Buck's joyful surprise, a work train had arrived from Key West and a temporary facility to feed emergency crews was in operation. He had his first warm meal in almost two days. After briefing railway personnel on the damage up the line and the situation at Long Key, he and Mike boarded the train. An hour and a half later they were in Key West, walking down Eaton Street toward the Bahama House.[10]

It was late afternoon, and the sky was populated with fast-moving clouds that seemed to be trying to catch up with the hurricane that had passed north of the island two days before. Tremendous anxiety had been building among the townsfolk as news of catastrophic damage and hundreds of deaths on the Upper Florida Keys trickled in via radios and the telephone and telegraph lines to Havana, the only ones still operating.

At 730 Eaton Street, Lindy had still not heard from her husband or received any information about the situation at Long Key. Family members had come over to the Bahama House to comfort her and to be there should grim news of her husband's fate arrive. She had been successful so far in concealing from her children the growing fear she felt as each hour passed.

Pat Duane and the husband of one of Lindy's cousins sat in rocking chairs on the front porch. The family often gathered there during the late afternoon, people-watching and relaxing. As she peered over the porch railing, the second-grader saw a man with a dog on the far side of the street about half a block away walking toward the house. He was clad in an undershirt and long khaki pants that were torn and soiled. As he continued in her direction, she noticed the uncombed hair, cheek stubble, and tired gait characteristic of the derelicts that hung around the waterfront bars on Caroline Street one block away. She would not have paid any further attention to him had it not been for the white dog with black patches that was staying close to the man's side; the dog looked like Mike. The man raised his head and saw her.

The fatigue on his face was instantly replaced by a familiar smile, and Pat Duane realized she was looking at her father. Seventy-five years later she recalled the scene on that memorable Wednesday.

> I think, at 7 years old, I didn't understand the tragedy that my family was going through. On this particular afternoon my mother's cousins Julia, Janeice, and Julia's husband, Charles Hogeboom, had come to visit the family. The ladies were all inside. I was sitting outside on the downstairs front porch with Charles who was telling me funny stories to make me laugh. We were using the front (Eaton Street) entrance at this time. There were about 4 or 5 rocking chairs for the usual afternoon gathering. I'm sure I had been to school that day, so it was probably around 5 o'clock. My attention was drawn to a man and a dog coming down Eaton Street about in the middle of the block on the opposite side from my house. I screamed to Charles, "Here comes Daddy!" He patted my head and softly said to me, "Hush, child." But he looked in the direction I was pointing, jumped out of his chair and went inside yelling, "Buck is coming! Buck is coming!" Then pandemonium broke loose.
>
> Daddy made it to the steps and collapsed with Mother holding him, and he cried and cried and cried. I believe that everyone shed tears of joy at that moment.[11]

To say that Buck was glad to be home would be a gross understatement. Forty-eight hours earlier, he and Mike had been battling the fury of one of the most powerful hurricanes to make landfall in the Florida Keys. That they were alive was amazing; that they had no significant injuries was a miracle. It was not long before the uncertainty of the future began to gnaw away the joy of his homecoming.

14

After the Storm

> The Fishing Camp here where I am the Caretaker is nothing but a mass of wreckage. My lowest Barometer reading was 26.98—This at 10:20 P.M. Sept. 2nd. The lull or Calm lasted a timed 55 minutes, 9:20 P.M. to 10:15 P.M. During lull there was always a very light Breeze—somewhat shifting, Sky clear, stars shining brightly, water was a terrible sight to see on Ocean side—Never will I forget the water raising—No not a Wave but looked just like the Vaccum drew it right up—Then let go—raising verry, very fast—Then it began to Pound—Very interesting these storms and have learned that this last kind are ones to avoid in the future—but who knows.
>
> I wish this could be made some kind of a real weather station. I'd like to have the job down here as I'm very, very interested. This was my seventh Hurricane that I came thru and the worst—if there happens to be such a word.
>
> —James Duane to Ernest Carson, September 14, 1935

On Wednesday morning, September 4, 1935, at about the same time that Buck started hiking to Marathon, a Coast Guard seaplane took off from its base at Dinner Key near Miami and began the first aerial inspection of the Florida Keys following the storm. Bad weather had thwarted earlier attempts to launch the mission. The reconnaissance flight provided the first authoritative information of the horrific destruction on the islands between Key Largo and Key Vaca.

The evacuation of survivors was made the first priority, a task that rough seas, missing navigation aids, and lack of communications made difficult. The disposal of the dead quickly became an imperative as decomposition accelerated by the tropical heat caused bodies to swell and become biological bombs. The scope of the operation is summarized in a report sent to President Roosevelt on Sunday, September 8, 1935:

> On Wednesday morning [September 4, 1935] Lieutenant Olson in the Coast Guard seaplane made the first airplane trip over the keys. The village at Islamorada was completely demolished. Boats were dispatched to all points where living persons had been observed and by Wednesday night it was reported that all injured and able bodied who wished to leave the keys had been evacuated. The Coast Guard, pleasure boats, and fishermen volunteered in the removal of all persons. On Thursday, the National Guard, Florida Emergency Relief Administration relief workers, Civilian Conservation Corps boys from a nearby camp and volunteers entered the keys at various points to remove the dead.
>
> . . . On Friday, approximately 800 men were operating in various parts of the keys removing bodies. On Saturday between 1,000 and 1,200 men continued this work. Wherever it is possible to place the body in a wooden box and bury boxes at suitable sites, this is being done. Wherever this is not possible, the bodies are being cremated.
>
> . . . The work of disposing of all bodies will proceed as rapidly as possible and will become more efficient as the organization is perfected. It is expected that all but the most inaccessible bodies will be disposed of by Sunday night, September 8. Work will continue, however, until all bodies are disposed of.[1]

The death toll on the islands from Key Largo to Lower Matecumbe was staggering. On the third and fourth days following the storm a total of 124 bodies were recovered and taken to the mainland for burial; thereafter, removal of the rapidly decomposing remains to the mainland was stopped due to public health concerns. Almost 300 bodies were cremated in the Florida Keys. A total of 485 bodies were reported to have been recovered by April 1936. The total number of people swept to sea could never be accurately determined.[2]

The crew that flew the Coast Guard's reconnoitering flight apparently did not observe any survivors at Long Key. Although Buck Duane arrived at Marathon the same afternoon and informed the authorities of the situation at the camp, a boat was not immediately dispatched to the island. This was most likely due to a matter of priorities and the lack of a craft of sufficient size to evacuate the survivors. Finally on Friday, the fifth day after the hurricane's passage, the yacht *Sue J* appeared at the west end of Long Key.

The *Sue J* was a sturdy craft built in 1931 by the Wheeler Shipbuilding Corporation of New York, a shipyard known for the wooden-hull sub chasers it produced during the Great War. With a length of 65 feet and a 16-foot beam, the *Sue J* had the lines of the speedy patrol boats, and her twin diesel engines made the yacht very fast. The vessel was also a floating radio station, having been equipped by her owner, Jesse Jay, with a high-fidelity short-wave transmitter and antennae expressly for broadcast purposes.

Jay, who was the general manager of radio station WIOD, the National Broadcasting Company's Miami affiliate, had obtained federal permission to make a special live, coast-to-coast broadcast from alongside the *Dixie,* a 426-foot Morgan Line steamship with more than 350 passengers and crew onboard that had been stranded by the hurricane on a reef off Key Largo. After taking aboard supplies for delivery to Red Cross field workers, Jay and his crew departed Miami early Wednesday afternoon and proceeded through very rough seas to the liner's location. They arrived the next morning just as the transfer of the passengers and most of the crew was being completed.[3]

Clinging to a stanchion as the rough seas tossed the yacht to and fro, Jay described the scene for seven minutes to a national audience before static from adverse atmospheric conditions became so bad that the network terminated the broadcast. The *Sue J* then continued down the Keys, stopping at Lower Matecumbe Key and Marathon to deliver the Red Cross supplies. After spending Thursday night at Marathon, the motor yacht proceeded to Long Key.[4]

The *Sue J* made a cautious approach to the island. The normally crystal-clear water was still clouded with sediment, making it difficult to judge the depth of the water and to see any submerged debris lurking in the murky water. Charts were of little use; navigational aids marking the channels had been swept away, and it was probable that the contours of the bottom had been changed by the water that had surged through the area. Making just enough speed to maintain steerageway, the captain felt his way, hoping the wood-planked hull would clear any unseen rocks or other hazards.

Scanning the shore with his binoculars, Jay was appalled by what he saw. Only a few tall palms remained of the lush grove that had covered the area. Mounds of splintered wood and twisted metal were interspersed with the shells of cottages canted in various positions, an impressive contorted monument to the savage power that had swept the place on Labor Day. There was little left that identified the wreckage as the remains of a resort. Since the marina dock was gone, the vessel made its way to the bay side of the concrete bulkhead of the East Approach.[5]

This aerial photograph taken three days after the storm shows the total devastation of the camp. Significant objects and landmarks have been marked by numbers and are identified below. The page numbers next to some entries refer to close-up views that appear elsewhere in this chapter. 1. Pompano—manager's house, p. 142; 2. lodge, pp. 143–44; 3. stranded barge, p. 144; 4. manager's office, p. 143; 5. dining hall site, p. 151; 6. post office; 7. caretaker's house site; 8. train station site, pp. 148–49; 9. gasoline tank, p. 146; 10. wrecked boat, p. 146; 11. cypress water tanks, p. 150; 12. exposed tunnel; 13. gas plant wreckage, p. 145; 14. boats *Dolphin* and *Mohican*, p. 147; 15. steel water tank, p. 145; 16. Long Key Viaduct. Photograph courtesy of Jerry Wilkinson.

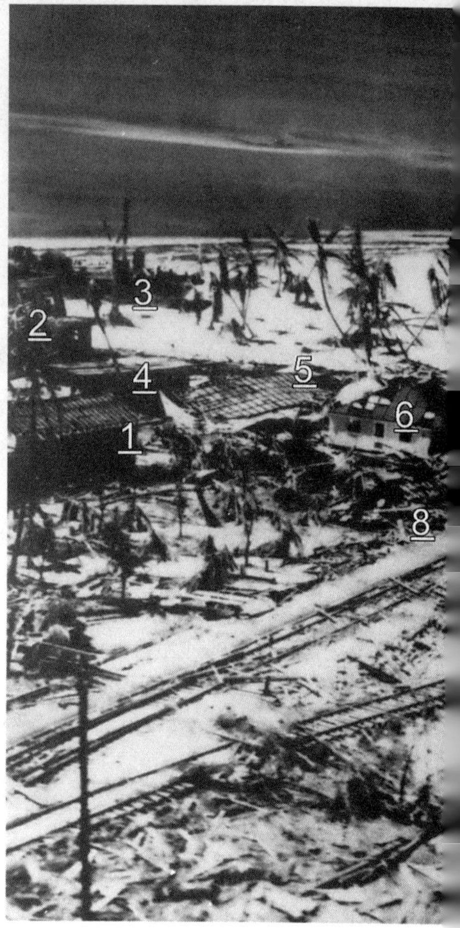

As he came ashore, Jay was greeted by the fifteen adults and four children who had stayed on the island when Duane hiked to Marathon. In an article written for the *Miami Daily News*, Jay reported: "Certainly there was no trace of the once-peaceful sportsman's paradise at Long Key, other than the complete wreckage of its hotels, cottages, tanks, railroad station, twisted steel and even small guide boats."[6]

The radio station manager and his party trudged through the debris and discovered a curious situation. At the demolished railroad station, the track had been twisted and rolled toward the ocean side onto the platform. West of the station, the twisted ribbon of rails and ties continued to stray toward the ocean all the way up to the abutment of the viaduct, where the track had been pushed 50 feet away from its roadbed and terminated in a ragged end dangling over the water.

In the opposite direction, fewer than 30 feet east of the station, there was a segment of track that appeared not to have been disturbed at all by the wind and surging water and lay on the centerline of its roadbed just as it had for a quarter of a century. Closer inspection showed that the rails were discolored, having a bluish-black hue as if subjected to intense heat and the ties under them were charred. This condition persisted for 780 feet eastward, at which point the track began to spiral off the roadbed toward the bay side.[7]

Knowing that the wind moves counterclockwise around the center of a hurricane and that the storm approached the Florida Keys from the ocean side, Jay concluded that the scorched segment could mean only one thing. "The tracks on the upper end of Long Key at one point were twisted first in one direction and then at an opposite direction," he wrote, "indicating to our minds that the exact center of the storm had passed here." The layman's conclusion did not influence the Weather Bureau. After analyzing the meteorological data, the weathermen determined that the center of the hurricane passed over Craig, 6 miles east of Long Key.[8]

As the Long Key survivors were being evacuated, the Flagler system had begun assessing the operational impact of the storm. The Florida East Coast Railway had been the umbilical cord that supplied potable water and provisions to all Flagler facilities on the islands between the mainland and Key West. Only the first 35 miles of track of the Key West Extension, from Florida City on the mainland to Tavernier on Key Largo, were usable. Restoration of service beyond that point would require many months and millions of dollars. In the meantime, decisions had to be made regarding the station agents, pumpers, maintenance crews, and other personnel who had been working in the Keys. For the Florida East Coast Hotel Company, the personnel decisions were made easier because the Long Key Fishing Camp was destroyed during the off-season and most of the staff was already off the payroll. The off-season staff was minimal, and all were let go except for Buck.[9]

This photograph was taken from the roof of the post office looking east. The building in the foreground is the manager's bungalow, the Pompano. Courtesy of Patricia J. Duane.

The poststorm view from atop the post office looking south toward the lodge, which is at the top right. Courtesy of Patricia J. Duane.

The decision of the people who had taken refuge in the lodge to relocate during the calm of the hurricane's eye proved to be a good one; the pile of wreckage in the center of this photograph is all that was left of the building. The intact building on the right is the manager's office. A stranded barge can be seen through the palm trees to the left of the lodge. Courtesy of Patricia J. Duane.

This close-up view of the lodge taken from the post-office roof shows the catastrophic damage it sustained. Courtesy of Patricia J. Duane.

The barge stranded on the beach just west of the lodge is believed to have been moored to the seawall on the bay side of the East Approach when it broke loose and was carried by the surging water over the fill. Courtesy of Patricia J. Duane.

The small building that housed the acetylene gas generator was buried with debris. Courtesy of Patricia J. Duane.

The elevated steel water tank succumbed to the onslaught of wind and waterborne debris. Courtesy of Patricia J. Duane.

The large gasoline storage tank that had been strapped to concrete pillows on the shore near the marina dock was ripped loose and came to rest against the mainline roadbed. Courtesy of Patricia J. Duane.

One of the camp's cabin cruisers rests on the railroad embankment with its fighting chairs still bolted to the cockpit floor and the anchor on the forward deck remaining in its brackets. Courtesy of Patricia J. Duane.

The *Dolphin* and *Mohican* ended up together in a pile of debris near the cypress water tanks. The *Mohican* was one of the six cabin cruisers designed and built in 1919 specifically for fishing in the Gulf Stream. Its superior freeboard and heft are evident compared to the smaller cabin cruiser. Courtesy of Patricia J. Duane.

Although the marina dock was washed away and the buildings ashore were demolished, the old marine railway winch that was used to haul boats out of the water stayed in place. Courtesy of Patricia J. Duane.

The incredible force exerted by the surging water and the debris it carried can be seen in this photograph taken from the east side of the train station platform looking west. The surge came from the right (bay side) flowing toward the left, lifting the track with ties still attached off its roadbed and twisting it like a ribbon toward the south. On the left are the remains of the station; on the right is the marina's gasoline storage tank. Courtesy of Patricia J. Duane.

This view from the west side of the train station looking toward the east shows how the rails and ties were completely flipped over onto the station platform. Courtesy of Patricia J. Duane.

East of the station where the wood-planked platform transitioned to a paved apron, the track remained on its roadbed, but portions of the ties were charred and the rails exhibited the dark tint of steel exposed to extreme heat. Further east of the burnt segment, the track had been lifted off its bed and pushed in a spiral toward Florida Bay. One observer considered this proof that the exact center of the hurricane's eye passed over Long Key because the track was twisted in opposite directions on either side of the burnt section. Courtesy of the Monroe County Public Library.

The hotel company had the caretaker return to the island to discourage looters and to salvage records and high-value items. After spending a few days in Key West, Buck arranged for a friend named Mickey to take him and Mike back to the island via speedboat. The arrangement provided for Mickey to periodically return with mail and supplies.[10]

In a letter written at Long Key twelve days after the storm, Duane told Walter Bennett, the head of the Jacksonville hurricane center: "The fishing camp is totally demolished. I am here as Caretaker pending orders from headquarters." It was a dicey situation. Buck had a rifle, camera, his dog, camping equipment, and canned goods. The site was littered with broken glass, boards with protruding nails, and sharp metal. Unstable remnants of buildings and piles of wreckage could kill or trap him. He had no way of communicating with anyone; if he was injured or pinned under a collapsing wall, he'd just have to wait for Mickey when he made his run with mail and supplies.[11]

At first there were things to be done; set up the camp, scrounge some furniture, and jury-rig some amenities such as a shower under the large elevated cypress water tank that still contained some freshwater. With the ever-faithful

Only one of the two large cypress water tanks remained on its legs. The tanks were used to store potable water unloaded from tanks on flatcars. After the storm, the residual freshwater in the tank was tainted with salt water, but it still provided a refreshing shower for Buck Duane. Courtesy of Patricia J. Duane.

Some buildings such as the one shown here appeared to be intact, but they were so full of seaweed and debris that they could not be entered. Courtesy of Patricia J. Duane.

Buck Duane was directed by the Florida East Coast Hotel Company to return to Long Key to protect the destroyed camp from looters while its future was decided. He hired a friend with a speedboat to take him to the island and make periodic visits to bring mail and supplies. In this photograph, the friend, Mickey (last name unknown), stands before a panorama of wrecked buildings and broken palm trees. Courtesy of Patricia J. Duane.

Buck and usable dinnerware he found in the debris of the dining hall and kitchen. The caretaker was authorized to keep many of the items he salvaged. Courtesy of Patricia J. Duane.

Mike at his side, he patrolled the site, clearing paths through the debris to make getting around easier and searching for items to salvage. The company had told Buck that he could keep any household or personal-use items he found. Sometimes Mickey would spend several days at Long Key working with Buck to dig through the wreckage. Repairable furniture, unbroken china, and such were bundled up and taken back to town on the speedboat. One of the prized items found was a fine tea service retrieved unscathed from the wreckage of the countess's cottage.

He also found some of the blue marbles, or "puries," that his daughter had admired scattered among the debris and filled a small cloth bag with them. Pat was thrilled when he gave her the bag, and the blue puries became one of her prized possessions.[12]

The Wahoo, the house built for the Countess of Suffolk, was torn apart during the storm. In the foreground, salvaged chairs and an electric reading lamp with bulb intact look to be in good condition. In the background, a china cabinet loaded with dinnerware reposes in its corner with a lampshade nearby. Courtesy of Patricia J. Duane.

This photograph provides further evidence that some of the bungalows had electrical power in 1935. In the foreground on the left is a salvaged oscillating electric fan, while a conduit and junction box hang overhead. Courtesy of Patricia J. Duane.

The physical conditions were rough, but the worst thing Buck had to contend with was uncertainty and loneliness. On September 25, 1935, he wrote Bennett: "I note your statement as to equipment at Long Key. Will advise as soon as I know what conditions will exist here. Things are very lonely here now—dog & speedboat only friends." He added below his signature the title "Caretaker of 'Wreckage Key.'"[13]

The Flagler interests continued to ponder whether the Key West Extension should be restored or abandoned. The Florida East Coast Railway had declared bankruptcy and been in receivership since September 1931 so the company was not free to make major expenditures even if it had the resources.

The home of the Countess of Suffolk was furnished with works of art and fine furniture. On the right, a painting still in its frame hangs on the wall while a comfortable sofa and chairs appear to be unharmed on the left. Courtesy of Patricia J. Duane.

Although the Key West Extension had been in operation for more than twenty-five years, it had never been a financial success. Maintenance, especially on the metal bridges, was very expensive and had increased dramatically as the system aged.

The railroad ferry service to Cuba had been a reliable source of revenue and would have been profitable but for the soaring costs of maintaining the line to Key West. The idea of relocating the ferry service to a port on the mainland had been considered for some years prior to the Labor Day Hurricane, but taking such action would have removed the only significant income-producing component of the line and triggered the closing of the Key West Extension. This in turn would have had the politically unacceptable consequence of dooming federal and state efforts to resuscitate the economic vitality of Monroe County and Key West.

The destruction of a significant portion of the line by natural forces changed everything. Now the relocation of the ferry terminal to the mainland and the restoration of the flow of goods between the United States and Cuba had become an undertaking in the national interest. Within three weeks after the

Labor Day hurricane's passage, an announcement was made that the ferry landing at Key West would be relocated to a port on the mainland. Six weeks later the ferry facility at Key West was stripped and the equipment moved to a newly constructed terminal at Port Everglades in Fort Lauderdale. Relieved of the burden of the Extension's costs, the ferry service to Cuba began generating much-needed revenue for the bankrupt company.[14]

Before the heavy steel ramps and other equipment of the ferry facility were dismantled, operable rolling stock on the Lower Keys portion of the Extension was collected and loaded onto ferries for transfer to the mainland. Although there was no announcement that the line would not be restored, it had become clear to Buck and others that there would be no rail service on the Keys for a long time, maybe never. This being the case, his presence at Long Key was pointless. Any further removal of salvageable material from the island would require the use of heavy equipment and a crew of men. Looting was possible, but the pickings would be slim as items of value that could easily be recovered had been removed or had been ruined by exposure to sun and rain.

Staying on the island was becoming more difficult each day. Without the railroad, the Long Key Fishing Camp would not be rebuilt; he had to face the

Amid the wreckage of the Wahoo protrudes the distinctive circular floor of an outdoor shower built for the countess between the bungalow and beach. On the right in the foreground is a coconut, one of thousands that the wind sent flying with lethal force. Courtesy of Patricia J. Duane.

Mike had been the Duane family's dog for several years when the storm occurred. He had stayed at Long Key except for the time he went with Buck to Key West after the storm. He was a faithful watchdog and companion for the caretaker, but not long after this photograph was taken something happened to Mike that caused him to stalk and threaten his owner. Shooting him was one of the hardest things Buck had to do. Courtesy of Patricia J. Duane.

reality that his time as a Flagler system employee was running out. The only thing that made life tolerable at Long Key now was his constant companion, Mike. Mike was someone to talk to, to acknowledge his kindness, and to protect him. Buck could sleep soundly knowing that if any varmints or intruders were about the dog would let him know.

It was a good relationship until the day the dog's behavior suddenly began to change. He became wary of Buck, looking at the caretaker as if his master was a stranger. Not long thereafter, Mike attacked Buck. He fended off the dog and was not physically hurt. He did not know if it was rabies, but Buck realized he might not be as fortunate if there was another attack, and he knew what he had to do. With a heavy heart he hunted down and shot his only friend on the island.

Just before Thanksgiving, Mickey arrived with a letter from the Florida East Coast Hotel Company notifying Buck of his termination. He packed up his gear and climbed aboard the speedboat. As they raced over the multihued waters, the island receded astern, their wake stretching back toward the Long Key Fishing Camp as it began to fade away.

Epilogue

During the mid-1930s, the Great Depression was winding down as unrest overseas began to signal that another global conflict was brewing. The destruction inflicted by the 1935 Labor Day Hurricane compounded the economic distress rampant in the Florida Keys, but it also paved the way for changes that would eventually bring a new level of prosperity to the region. The people who had been involved with the Long Key Fishing Camp, including some of the guests, had to cope with its sudden demise and move on with their lives.

The Duane Family

Buck Duane must have felt a sense of relief upon being released from the depressing duty of guarding the wrecked fishing camp, but that would have been quickly replaced by the realization that he was unemployed just before Christmas in a town that had declared insolvency the previous year and where his wife was about to deliver their third child. Fortunately, he found work with a plumbing company.

About two weeks before Christmas 1935, Lindy gave birth to their son. According to his sister, the joy of his arrival was tempered when it was learned that his umbilical cord had been wrapped tightly around his neck, reducing the flow of blood to his brain. At first the effects were not noticeable, but as the months went by, it became clear that his development was not normal. Mentally disabled, he would require extensive care for the rest of his life.

In 1937, a massive military buildup began in Key West that transformed the town. By 1939, the reactivation of the Naval Station had created hundreds of jobs. James Duane went back to work for the Navy as a civilian, testing and refilling fire extinguishers. A federal civil service employee for twenty-six years, he was a plumber at the Naval Hospital when he retired in 1966 after suffering a stroke.

According to his daughter Pat, his experience with the 1935 Labor Day Hurricane changed him. "For many years after that when Daddy would talk about the hurricane, when he got to the 'coming home' part, he would choke up. Every year when hurricanes were reported, he became very up-tight."

Buck died in 1979 and Lindy in 2001. "We scattered their ashes where they had spent their happiest days together," said Pat, "at the site of the Long Key Fishing Camp."[1]

During the 1935 Labor Day Hurricane, Buck kept the people at Long Key together and moved them into the sturdiest building he could think of, the bungalow built for the Countess of Suffolk. Had he not done so, it is probable that many of them, perhaps all, would not have survived the storm. His clear thinking and leadership during the chaos of the storm were never recognized by the community or the Flagler system.

The Blue Puries

When her father returned from Long Key in 1935 and gave Pat Duane the blue puries that he had salvaged from the wreckage of the fishing camp, they immediately became her most-prized possession. She proudly showed them to her friends, and all who saw the gleaming orbs were impressed with their clarity and beauty. It became known that she owned some of the finest marbles on the island.

One day in 1937 William "Billy" Freeman Jr., who was about her age and lived next door, invited her to play marbles with him, his brother, and two of their chums from the Catholic school. Nine-year-old Pat was flattered since most of the time he scarcely acknowledged her existence, and she paid no heed to the requirement that she play with the blue puries. She went over to his yard with her bag of marbles in hand and joined the four boys kneeling on a bare patch of ground around the required playing circle that had been freshly etched with a stick.

With Billy were his younger brother David and their school pals, Patrick and Gregory Hemingway, the author's sons, who were the same ages respectively as the Freeman boys. "It didn't take long for them to get all the marbles," lamented Pat when interviewed in 2010, adding, "They 'stole' all my beautiful puries!" Forty years after the "theft," Billy became the sheriff of Monroe County and served in that position with distinction from 1976 to 1989.[2]

Henry Flagler

Despite his complaint that he would have been richer if he had not invested in Florida, Henry Flagler did very well financially. When he died in 1913, his estate was estimated to be worth $100 million, approximately equivalent to $2.4 billion now.[3]

On May 20, 1913, the *St. Augustine Evening Record* carried the following announcement: "Every wheel on the Florida East Coast Railway system will cease turning tomorrow afternoon at 3 o'clock for a period of ten minutes. This is during the hour of the funeral. No matter where it is every train will stop for that period of time as a token of respect for the departed great man who made the Florida East Coast Railway system possible."[4]

The Remarkable Schutt Family

The Schutt family began what would become a multigenerational record of successful resort management in America when Peter Schutt opened the first hotel in the Catskill Mountains in 1800. His descendants, including Louis P. "L. P." Schutt and his family, carried on the tradition. In 1898, after operating resorts in the Catskills, L. P. accepted a position with Henry Flagler's Florida East Coast Hotel Company and worked with H. E. Bemis, manager of the Royal Victoria in Nassau. In later years, Schutt's three sons received their hotel training under Bemis, starting at the bottom.

The zenith of the family's resort-management endeavors came in 1931, when L. P. was manager of the Casa Marina Hotel at Key West; his oldest son, George, was manager of the Long Key Fishing Camp; his second son, Peter, was manager of the Hotel Charlotte Harbor at Punta Gorda on Florida's west coast; and his youngest son, Frank, was manager of the Hotel Peabody in Memphis.[5]

Frank Schutt is credited with having started the tradition of ducks swimming in the fountain of the Peabody's lobby. He and a friend were returning from a hunting trip in 1932 when they thought it would be amusing to place their live decoys (ducks with clipped wings) in the massive travertine marble fountain that forms the centerpiece of the two-story lobby. The guests were so delighted that the Peabody ducks became as much a part of the hotel as the magnificent fountain and remain so to this day.[6]

In 1934, a year after L. P. Schutt's death, the Florida East Coast Hotel Company agreed to reopen the Casa Marina in an attempt to help revive the Key West economy. Peter Schutt succeeded his father as manager of the Casa Marina and presided over the grand reopening on New Year's Eve. He remained in that position through the end of World War II.[7]

Soon after the highway was completed in 1938, George Schutt became manager of a fishing camp that opened briefly at Pigeon Key. The Pigeon Key Fishing Camp was only 21 miles west of Long Key, and offered almost the same access to large game fish; however, the entire island was one-fifth the size of the Long Key Fishing Camp and lacked amenities such as a spacious lodge, white-sand beach, and large marina. Tucked under the Seven-Mile Bridge and devoid of the natural beauty and serenity that characterized Long Key, the Pigeon Key camp was basically a boat-rental and tackle shop that catered to the motoring public. Schutt had no chance of attracting his former elite clientele to such a place, and the camp rapidly failed. By January 1940, George had moved on to work with R. C. Perky, who was creating an upscale resort on Sugarloaf Key, 14 miles east of Key West.[8]

The Countess of Suffolk

Marguerite "Daisy" Hyde Leiter became the Countess of Suffolk and Berkshire in 1904, when she married the 19th Earl of Suffolk and the 12th Earl of Berkshire, Henry Molyneux Paget Howard. When he was killed in 1917, their eleven-year-old son Charles became the 20th Earl of Suffolk and the 13th Earl of Berkshire and Daisy became the Dowager Countess of Suffolk and Berkshire. She continued to be referred to as the Countess of Suffolk for convenience.

When Charles married in 1934, his bride became the Countess of Suffolk and Berkshire. His mother, who had been residing with Charles and Lieutenant Colonel Gillett at Charlton Park, bought a nearby manor previously owned by the Baron of Redlynch, into which she and Gillett moved.[9]

Charles was a scientist and during World War II served in the Directorate of Scientific Research of the Ministry of Supply as a liaison with the French scientific community. Just before the Germans invaded France, Lord Suffolk and his private confidential secretary, Eileen Beryl Morden, arranged for the removal to England of sophisticated machine tools, $10 million worth of industrial diamonds, fifty top French scientists, and heavy water, the latter produced in Norway by the Germans for nuclear research. Upon his return to England, Lord Suffolk formed an unexploded bomb demolition team consisting of himself, Morden, and his chauffeur. They were killed in May 1941 while attempting to defuse their thirty-fifth bomb.[10]

The manor in Redlynch Park was Daisy's home in England from 1934 until 1967. She died a year later in a hospital at Lancaster, California, at the age of eighty-nine after being stricken while aboard her private plane as it was flying from San Francisco to Tucson, Arizona, her primary residence in the United States.[11]

The Cardezas

Charlotte Drake Cardeza, a.k.a. Lady Cardeza, passed away in 1939 at her home. She was ninety-five and had been confined to her mansion in Philadelphia for several years due to declining health. In 1941, her son Thomas Drake Martinez Cardeza and his wife, Mary, established the Cardeza Foundation for Hematologic Research at Thomas Jefferson University as a memorial to his mother. Mary had developed a blood illness in the late 1930s and was being treated by a doctor at the medical college of the University. Mary Racine Cardeza died at the Jefferson Hospital in 1943 at the age of sixty-three. When her husband died in 1952, he left $5 million to the college and hospital with instructions that it be used for hematology research. According to the University, the financial support provided by the Cardezas has "enabled creation of one of the premier academic hematology programs in the world."[12]

Lou Gehrig

Just as he had witnessed the powerful manta ray fade slowly away into the deep-blue waters of the Gulf Stream in the spring of 1935, Lou Gehrig saw his strength and stamina slowly slip away from his body. Bouts of fatigue and "lumbago" attacks began to reoccur. By the midpoint of the 1938 season his performance on the field had noticeably diminished. He was tired and was unable to restore his energy. The next summer doctors at the Mayo Clinic diagnosed him as having amyotrophic lateral sclerosis (ALS). The "Iron Horse" retired from baseball two days later. He died on June 2, 1941, at his home in New York City at the age of thirty-seven.[13]

Wallace Stevens

Beginning in 1922, when he became a charter member of the "Long Key Fishing Club of Atlanta," Wallace Stevens visited the camp almost every winter, usually in the company of one or more of his business associates. Stevens often went on to Key West and sometimes to Cuba, but Long Key, with its isolated beach and natural beauty, was like a rejuvenating tonic for him. Five months after the destruction of the fishing camp Wallace Stevens would want for its solace as never before. That was when he had a physical confrontation with Ernest Hemingway.

In February 1936, Stevens was in Key West and attended a party at a private home near the Casa Marina, where he was staying. Also at the party was Ernest Hemingway's sister Ursula. Her brother had moved to the Island City in 1928 and was living in a house near the lighthouse. The fifty-six-year-old Stevens, who true to form had had too much to drink, cornered Ursula and began lecturing her about his view of her brother's shortcomings, both as a writer and as a man. The obnoxious upbraiding persisted until the thirty-four-year-old woman burst into tears and fled the party. No specific incident was known to have triggered Stevens's denigration of the famous author.

Distraught, Ursula went directly to the Hemingway house and tearfully recounted the incident to Ernest. According to Hemingway, this was the third time Stevens had publicly made such remarks. Fed up, he left to confront the man.

In the meantime, Stevens was making his farewell remarks to anyone who cared to listen and in closing said that he wished Hemingway had been at the party so he could knock him out with one punch. With his friend Judge Powell, he made his way out the door, where he found a very agitated Hemingway arriving. It was dark and the street was wet from a passing shower. Stevens approached the object of his disdain and threw the first punch. He missed, and Hemingway reciprocated by knocking Stevens down several times. In an exchange of blows, Stevens did land one solid punch to Hemingway's jaw, breaking his own hand in two places but doing no noticeable damage to Hemingway. Although he was the larger of the two, the inebriated poet proved to be no match for an enraged author twenty years his junior.

According to Hemingway, his opponent was removed to his hotel and stayed in his room under the care of a nurse and doctor. Five days later, when his body and ego permitted, he went to the Hemingway home, where he apologized to Ursula and made peace with her brother. Stevens was concerned that the incident could have an adverse impact on his career with the Hartford, where he had recently been promoted to vice president, so all parties agreed that if anyone asked about Stevens's injuries, they would be attributed to a fall down the Key West lighthouse stairs; no mention would be made of his drunken brawl.

Wallace needed more time and seclusion to recuperate before returning to Connecticut. Since the Long Key Fishing Camp no longer existed, he went into seclusion at Pirate's Cove, a small-scale fishing camp on Sugarloaf Key rumored to be a favorite of gangsters seeking to avoid the public eye. The strategy of lying low and employing a cover story was apparently successful; Stevens remained an executive of the Hartford until he died of stomach cancer in 1955. Earlier that year he was awarded the Pulitzer Prize for his poetry.[14]

Benny Crowninshield

One of the memorable achievements of Benjamin W. Crowninshield was his inclusion in "The Bonefish Brigade," a satirical piece written by Zane Grey about the fishermen of the Long Key Fishing Camp. Benny enjoyed fishing, cooking, making money, and more fishing. A wise investor, he did well and was thrifty. When he died in 1953, he reportedly had a large box at his house overflowing with stock certificates. His personal checking account made up so much of a Massachusetts bank's assets that the financial institution did not want to transfer the funds when first requested by the executor of his estate in Florida. He was a faithful member of the Long Key Fishing Club throughout its existence and was greatly respected by Zane Grey and other sportfishermen for his skill with light tackle.[15]

Zane Grey

The Long Key Fishing Club's most famous president, Zane Grey, wrote eighty-nine books from 1903 to 1939, many of which became best sellers. While primarily known for his westerns, Grey also wrote books about hunting, fishing, and baseball, and authored six children's books. Twenty-seven million copies of his books had been sold by his sixty-seventh year, when he died of heart failure in 1939 at his home in Altadena, California. The endearment he felt for Long Key and the surrounding waters often comes through in his fish stories.[16]

A Continuous Highway and Water for the Keys

After the Labor Day Hurricane, Long Key remained isolated from the mainland for the better part of two years. By March 1936, the receivers of the Florida East Coast Railway obtained estimates ranging as high as $3.5 million to repair the hurricane damage sustained by the Key West Extension. There was no financial incentive for restoring rail service to Key West. In the years just prior to the storm, the Extension had been operating at an annual loss of more than $300,000. Furthermore, the Flagler system ferry service to Cuba was operating more profitably since being relocated from Key West to Port Everglades.

In the meantime, pressure was growing for the construction of a continuous highway over the idle railroad bridges. With the help of federal, state, and county agencies, a financing plan was developed, and by the summer of 1936, the Key West Extension property was transferred to a highway toll commission set up by the state on behalf of Monroe County. In return for the 122 miles of right-of-way and all improvements including the bridges, the Flagler system received $640,000 and forgiveness of $300,000 in state, city, and county taxes. The federal Public Works Administration provided a $3.6 million loan to the toll commission to fund the cash payment to the railroad and the cost of converting 40 miles of right-of-way to a highway, which would eliminate the need for ferries.[17]

Work began on Long Key and the other islands involved in November 1936. Debris was cleared, fill restored where needed, and a paved road was built over the route of the former mainline. With the exception of the small trestle at Snake Creek, the bridges and viaducts had suffered no structural damage. A new bridge was constructed at Snake Creek, and the narrow railroad bridges and viaducts were modified to accommodate two lanes of vehicular traffic. The work was completed by the end of March 1938.[18]

The new road was connected to the highway built in the 1920s, and although this made the highway continuous from the mainland to Key West, it was circuitous, especially in the Lower Keys, where the old road did not follow the railroad right-of-way. After fourteen years of service and exposure to the elements, the original road surface and wooden bridges of the old highway needed to be replaced. During World War II, the remainder of the Key West Extension mainline route was converted to a highway, providing a more direct road capable of carrying the heavy loads needed to support the military installations being reactivated and built at Key West.[19]

The rapid military buildup was extensive, and thousands of servicemen were stationed on the island. At its peak, the population of the Key West area more than doubled. The rapid increase in population produced shortages of potable water that threatened military readiness. Wells drilled on the island produced brackish water. The demand for freshwater was so great that it could not be met by storing rainwater in cisterns as had been the practice prior to the war. Consequently a pipeline was hastily constructed alongside the highway to bring potable water from wells on the mainland to Key West.[20]

The Long Key Viaduct, as shown in this view, was converted to a two-lane vehicular bridge as part of a project to make the highway continuous and eliminate the need for ferries. The ferry-less Overseas Highway was opened on March 30, 1938. Courtesy of the State Archives of Florida, *Florida Memory*, http://floridamemory.com.

After the war, as the armed forces began to demobilize, the military population in the Florida Keys was drastically reduced, releasing capacity in the potable water pipeline for civilian use. The end result was that all the islands that had been served by the railroad were not only accessible via a first-class highway but also had available a reliable source of freshwater. This infrastructure set the stage for a frenzy of land development, much of it dredge-and-fill, that would transform the Florida Keys physically, economically, and demographically during the latter half of the twentieth century.[21]

The Transformation of Long Key

The Florida East Coast Hotel Company had been trying to sell the land it owned at the wreckage-strewn west end of Long Key ever since the decision was made not to restore rail service to the Keys. Although the 45½-acre parcel included the former site of the fishing camp, 2,400 feet of beautiful beach, and more than 3,000 feet of bay front with a good depth of water, finding a buyer proved to be a challenge in an economy still recovering from the Great Depression and dealing with the uncertainty brought on by war. Finally, in June 1945, it was sold to Miami real estate speculator Scott Braznell for $35,000, or $769 per acre.[22]

Much of Long Key, including the former railroad right-of-way, remained in government hands. In September 1961, Monroe County sold to the State of Florida approximately 50 acres for one dollar, with the stipulation that the land be used "as fishing and camping areas and for other park and recreational purposes." This was the beginning of Long Key State Park. By 2004, the park had increased to 980 acres and included 1½ miles of shoreline on the bay side of the highway and 6 miles of shoreline on the ocean side.[23]

Some parcels along the highway at the northeast end of the island that had remained in private hands were developed into commercial and residential properties. Midway along the north shore, a 12.5-acre development was incorporated in 1963 as the City of Layton, population 184 per the 2010 census.[24]

The property formerly owned by the Florida East Coast Hotel Company was subdivided and now has about five hundred owners. The ocean side, where the fishing camp lodge and cottages once stood, is occupied by condominiums, townhouses, rental homes, and a few residences on relatively large waterfront lots. The bay side, with the exception of the extreme western 1.4 acres where the Edgewater Lodge sits, was intensively dredged and filled to create more land. To increase its market value, the site was laced with almost three-quarters of a mile of canals. The land was subdivided into more than

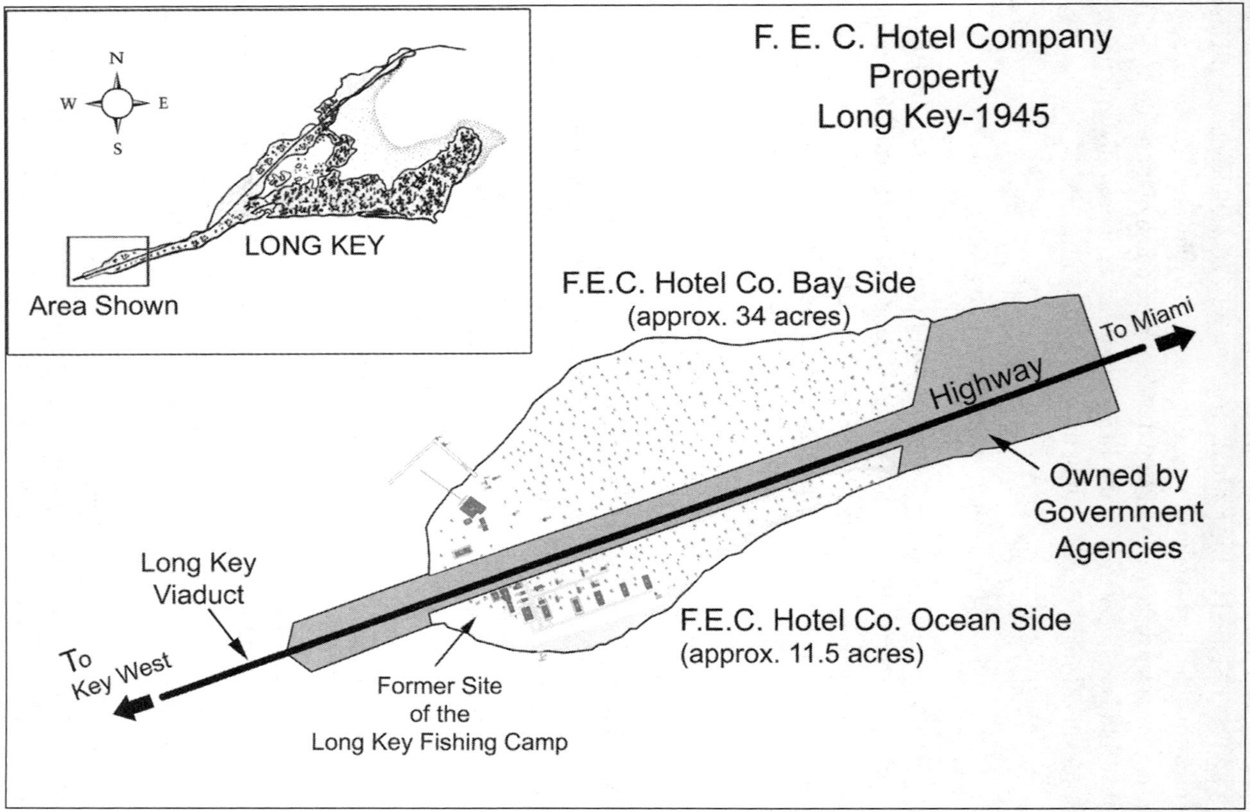

Long Key, showing property owned by the Florida East Coast Hotel Company in 1945. Map by Thomas Neil Knowles.

This 2006 photograph shows the former Florida East Coast Hotel Company property after sixty-one years of development. The area where the fishing camp used to be (*lower left*) is occupied on the bay side by a motel and private homes, and on the ocean side by a couple of homes and several large condominiums. Courtesy of the Monroe County property appraiser.

400 private lots, of which 44 are on the bay and 170 are on canals. The current value of the land and improvements is about $100 million.[25]

Epitaph

In 1936, Zane Grey wrote that it was sad that the Long Key Fishing Camp, with its rustic charm and unique sense of place, was lost forever but that "the long white winding lonely shore of coral sand, and the green surf, and the blue Gulf Stream will live in memory." There is no doubt that he spoke for all who had enjoyed the natural beauty and camaraderie of Long Key during the existence of its fishing camp. They would be pleased to know that most of the island is a state park dedicated to public outdoor recreation and conservation.[26]

This view of the long, winding beach framed by swaying palms and sparkling water as a train on the viaduct disappears into the blue horizon was one of many things that made the Long Key Fishing Camp a very special place. Courtesy of Patricia J. Duane.

Acknowledgments

Many people and institutions provided information, materials, or otherwise contributed to bringing this work to fruition. I especially appreciate Pat Duane giving me the opportunity to tell the story of her family's involvement with the Long Key Fishing Camp and for sharing her recollections of the good times and hardships they experienced during this dynamic period of Florida Keys history.

Others who have been of considerable help include: Tom Hambright, curator of the historical collection of the Monroe County Public Library; Jerry Wilkinson, president of the Historical Preservation Society of the Upper Keys; Susan Swiatoz, former archivist of the Flagler Museum; Mary Devine of the Boston Public Library; Bob Wolz of the Harry S. Truman Little White House in Key West; and the staff of the State of Florida Photographic Archives. Jim Gale, GIS technician at the Monroe County Property Appraisers Office, provided assistance with aerial photographs and GIS mapping. Dr. Joe Knetsch, research historian with the Division of State Lands, Florida Dept. of Environmental Protection, provided materials and information that were very helpful.

Authors Thomas Graham and David Nolan read the manuscript for the publisher and graciously made suggestions that enhanced the work. Richard Benham provided guidance on copyrights and permissions.

Dave Tranchand took on the tedious task of editing the manuscript and did his usual superb job. Larry Abele, who during his teen years fished from and slept under the Long Key Viaduct, provided assistance with the review of the book and has been a great source of encouragement.

I have enjoyed working with the staff and associates of the University Press of Florida. Their guidance and professional courtesy made the publication process much easier for me.

To some extent this was a family project. My sister, Joan Langley of the Wright Langley Archives, provided photographs and suggestions, and my brother David Knowles scanned some of the Duane photographs. Most of all I appreciate the unwavering support of my wife, Barbara, whose help and patience allowed me to finish this work.

Appendix

The Middle Keys Storm Surge

According to Gordon Dunn, one of the meteorologists at the Jacksonville Weather Bureau responsible for tracking the 1935 Labor Day hurricane, the severity of the damage done by the storm in the hardest-hit areas indicated maximum winds of 200–250 mph.[1]

The fierce wind was caused by the extremely low pressure that existed in the core of the storm, a condition that spawned another powerful force that was responsible for the greatest amount of damage and loss of life. While over the ocean, the low pressure created a dome of water that moved slightly ahead and to the right of the storm's path. Hardly noticeable in deep water, when the dome encountered the sheer walls of the reef lining the Florida Straits the water welled up and spread out. The U.S. Army Corps of Engineers determined that by the time the surge reached the railroad, it was a mass of water about 25 miles long with an average height of approximately 16 feet above mean sea level.[2]

The initial surge inundated the islands from the middle of Long Key to just north of the Tavernier train station on Key Largo as it flowed into the relatively shallow Florida Bay. Constrained by the islands along the eastern rim of the bay and the Everglades to the north, much of the excess water was driven by the wind to the west and south.

The islands of the Florida Keys crossed by the railroad form an arc with a north-south segment running from the southeastern tip of the mainline to Craig and an east-west segment running from Craig to Key West. The center of the hurricane crossed over Craig. As it moved into the bay, the counterclockwise wind spiraling about the center pushed the water over the islands of the Middle Florida Keys, from the west end of Long Key to milepost 470 at the eastern tip of Key Vaca, 4 miles east of Marathon.

The population of this area was sparse at the time, consisting of the people at Long Key and the section gang station at milepost 464 on Grassy Key. The

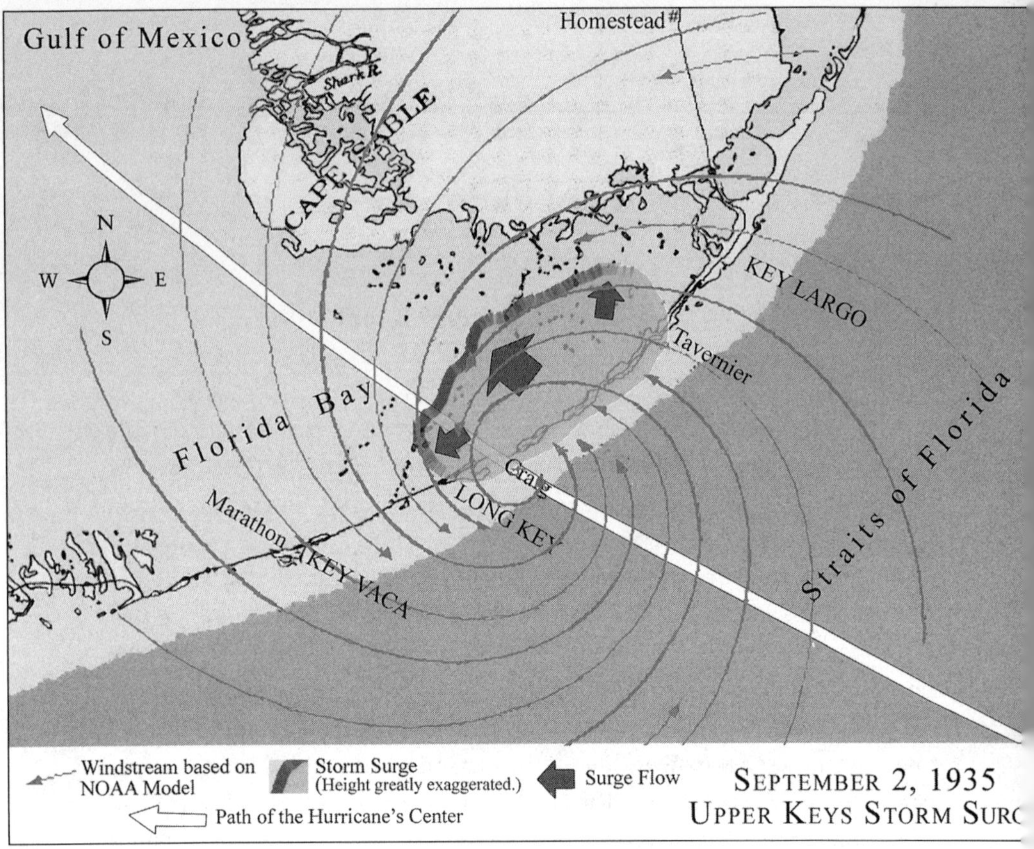

The initial storm surge came from the Florida Straits and swept across the islands from the midpoint of Long Key to the southwest end of Key Largo into Florida Bay. Map by Thomas Neil Knowles.

natural grade at the section gang station was about 7 feet above mean sea level; however, it was situated at the low point between two fills, causing the water flow to be concentrated on the station. Most of the station's inhabitants evacuated to Marathon and survived the storm. The four people who chose to stay at the station perished.[3]

The U.S. Army Corps of Engineers plotted storm surge heights on a Florida East Coast Railway roadbed profile chart for the Upper Keys (from Key Largo to Long Key). At Long Key, the plot ends just west of milepost 455, near the midpoint of island, at a height of 16 feet. The Upper Keys storm surge flowed from the ocean side to the bay side, after which there was a resurgence from the bay toward the ocean.

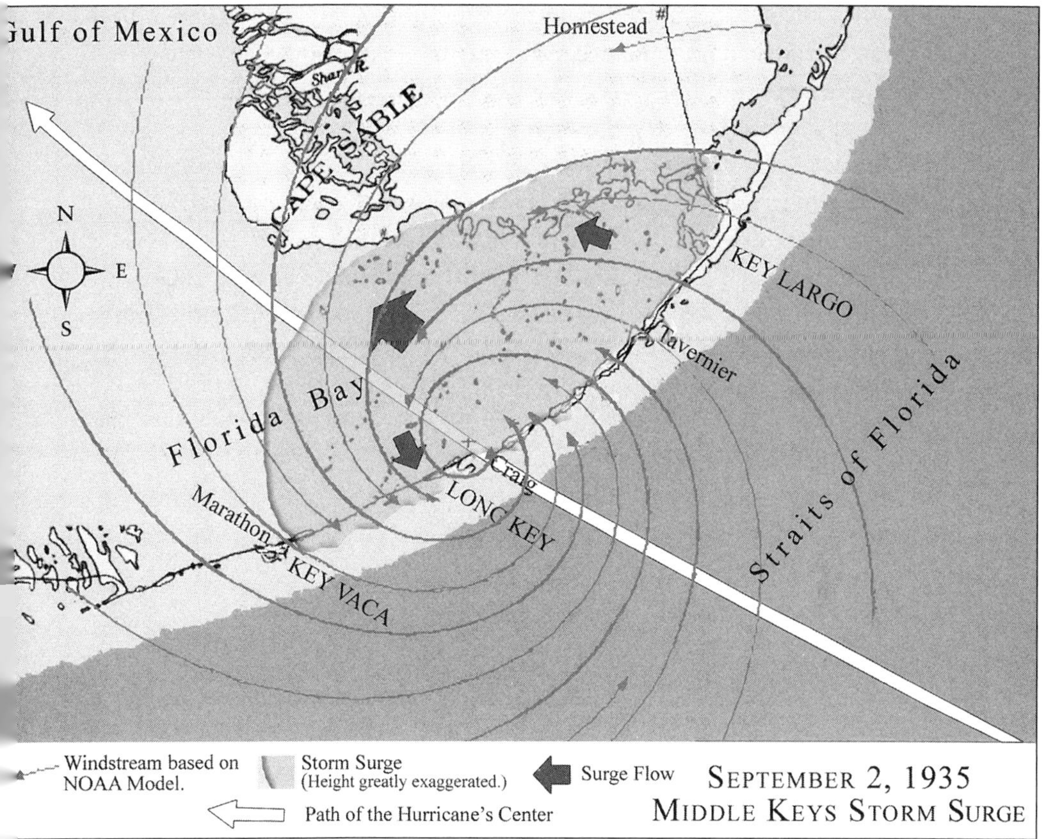

A secondary surge occurred when the spiraling winds of the hurricane pushed water in Florida Bay around the storm's center and over the islands from the midpoint of Long Key to the east end of Key Vaca. Map by Thomas Neil Knowles.

The height attained by the surge in the Middle Keys (from Long Key to Key Vaca) was not similarly documented by the Corps of Engineers; however, photographs of the damaged railroad and narrative reports clearly indicate the flow was from the bay toward the ocean.

The entire track across the Long Key Viaduct and other smaller viaducts to the west was stripped by the hurricane and later found submerged on the ocean side of the crossings. The maximum height of the track on the Long Key Viaduct was 31 feet above mean sea level; it is highly improbable that the surge reached this elevation. A more likely scenario is that the storm water in the Middle Keys reached a maximum height of approximately 10–15 feet above mean sea level and lifted the track and ties off the roadbed of the approaches enough to expose the underside to the wind, which then proceeded to peel them off the viaduct. Similar displacements of track and debris occurred down the line toward Key Vaca/Marathon, confirming that the Middle Keys flow was from the bay toward the ocean.

The surface wind of the hurricane was so powerful that granite ballast from the roadbed on the Long Key Viaduct was found on the platform of the Alligator Reef lighthouse 15 miles to the southeast. Poststorm surveys of the Middle Keys determined that 13.3 miles of the railroad was rendered inoperable with 65,800 cubic yards of fill being washed away and 11 miles of track either missing or being so twisted that it needed to be replaced. The damage done to the line in the Upper Keys was much worse.[4]

Notes

Prologue

1. Call, *The Concentration of Wealth*, 3 (number of millionaires in 1850); "American Millionaires," *Tribune Monthly*, June 1892, 3–4.

2. Phillips, *The Politics of Rich and Poor*, cited in http://everything2.com/title/What%2527s+a+Million%253F.

3. Josephson, *The Robber Barons*.

4. "The Wealthiest Americans Ever," *New York Times*, July 15, 2007, www.archive.org/details/cu31924029948258; LeFèvre, "Flagler and Florida," 181.

5. "Henry Flagler Left $75,000,000 Estate," *New York Times*, November 20, 1917.

Chapter 1. Why Did Henry Do It?

1. Chandler, *Henry Flagler*, 287–89; "Henry Flagler Left $75,000,000 Estate."

2. Chandler, *Henry Flagler*, 287–89.

3. Rockefeller, *Random Reminiscences*, 12.

4. Ibid., 13, 14.

5. Ibid., 10.

6. *Jacksonville News-Herald*, June 20, 1887.

7. Braden, *The Architecture of Leisure*, 93; Graham, "Henry M. Flagler's Hotel Ponce de Leon," 96–111.

8. Reynolds, *Standard Guide—St. Augustine*, 1890, 32–42.

9. Rockefeller, *Random Reminiscences*, 11.

Chapter 2. The Oversea Railroad, Long Key, and the Viaduct

1. Corliss, "Building the Overseas Railway," 3–6.

2. "A Keys Gazetteer," Florida International University Digital Collections Center, http://keys.fiu.edu/gazetteer/tr400.htm.

3. Iardella and Dorr, Extracts, 252–53.

4. Robison, "Henry Perrine," 16–24; Perrine, "Successive Crops of Cocoons in Tropical Florida," 566–67.

5. "A Letter by Dr. Perrine," *Tequesta* 1, no. 39 (1979): 29–33; Schene, "Indian Key," 1976, 3–27.

6. Dodge, "Subtropical Florida," 345–62.

7. Right of Way and Track Maps, Florida East Coast Railway Co., vol. 4, sheets 16 & 17.

8. *Florida East Coast Hotel Co. Map, 1923 Correction & Tracing*; "Long Key Fishing Camp Brings Price of $35,000," *Key West Citizen*, June 29, 1945.

9. Gallagher, *Florida's Great Ocean Railway*, 97–112, 181.

10. Corliss, "Building the Overseas Railway," 10–11.

11. Saunders, "The Wreck of Houseboat No. 4 October 1906," 15–21.

12. Paine, "Over the Florida Keys by Rail," 153; Corliss, "Building the Overseas Railway," 12.

13. Corliss, "Building the Overseas Railway," 10.

14. Staats, "The Transformation of the Florida East Coast," 263.

Chapter 3. From Work Camp to Fishing Camp

1. Knetsch, "The Business System of Henry Flagler," 68–84.

2. Mueller, "The FEC Steamship Company," 53; Corliss, "Henry M. Flagler: Railroad Builder," 202.

3. "Announcement Key West Extension of the Florida East Coast Railway Opened January 22nd 1912," Florida East Coast Railway, 1912.

4. Gallagher, *Florida's Great Ocean Railway*, 97; Chandler, *Henry Flagler*, 124–34.

5. "Louis P. Schutt, Hotel Man, Dies," *New York Times*, July 1, 1933; "Born to Their Profession," *Catskill Recorder* (Greene Co., N.Y.), June 5, 1931, 5.

6. "Long Key Fishing Camp—Improvements," MSS0027, Folder 8079, Florida East Coast Railway Over-sea Railroad Records, Henry Morrison Flagler Museum Archives, Palm Beach, FL. This undated, unsigned report is believed to have been prepared by L. P. Schutt for H. E. Bemis prior to November 18, 1908.

7. Newspaper articles about the Florida East Coast Railway copied by Fran & Rudy Atmos, provided by Jerry Wilkinson. The typed copies of the articles do not identify the newspaper or dates of publication.

8. *Florida Star* (Titusville), January 20, 1909, 8.

9. *Key West Citizen*, August 5, 1909.

10. "List of Hotels and General Information 1909–1910," Florida East Coast Railway, October 1909, 88–89.

11. "Announcement Key West Extension."

12. Grey, "Bonefish Brigade," 134.

13. Gruber, *Zane Grey*, 13.

Chapter 4. A Fishing Camp Extraordinaire

1. This description of the camp was developed from a Florida East Coast Hotel Company drawing dated April 14, 1917, and updated in 1923; the recollections of a caretaker's daughter who resided there during the summers of the early 1930s; and photographs from the State of Florida Photographic Archives, the Monroe County Public Library, and other sources. *Florida East Coast Hotel Co. Map of*

Part of Long Key, 1923 Correction & Tracing; Pat Duane, interviews by Thomas N. Knowles, 2010.

2. Right of Way and Track Maps, Florida East Coast Railway Co., sheets 16 & 17.

3. U.S. Army Corps of Engineers, "Chart of Hurricane of Sept. 2, 1935"; Right of Way and Track Maps, Florida East Coast Railway Co., sheet 17.

4. "U.S. Dept. of Agriculture, Weather Bureau, Temperature and Precipitation Data," in *Florida Hurricane Disaster*, 273.

5. Brazeau, *Parts of a World*, 98–99.

6. Pat Duane, interviews by Knowles, 2010.

7. *Florida East Coast Hotel Co. Map of Part of Long Key, 1923 Correction & Tracing*; Pat Duane, interviews by Knowles, 2010.

8. "Reduction In Ferry Trips Will Be Made," *Key West Citizen*, April 30,1935, 1; Right of Way and Track Maps, Florida East Coast Railway Co., sheets 14 & 21; Bethel, *First Overseas Highway to Key West, Florida*.

9. *Long Key Fishing Club, Season 1934–35*, 5, 7.

10. Pat Duane, interviews by Knowles, 2010.

11. Long Key Fishing Camp receipt dated March 26, 1917, Wright Langley Archives.

12. Wells, ed., "Council of Fire," 414.

13. *Long Key Fishing Club, Season 1934–35*, 7.

14. Reynolds, *The Standard Guide—Florida*, 72.

Chapter 5. The Long Key Fishing Club

1. Sutton, *The Silver Kings of Aransas Pass*, 256–64.

2. *New York Times*, March 10, 1912.

3. Information regarding the Long Key Fishing Club is from *Long Key Fishing Club, Season 1934–35*, 5, 10–11.

4. Sutton, *The Silver Kings of Aransas Pass*, 257.

Chapter 6. Sailfish and Boats

1. Dement, "Species Spotlight: Atlantic Sailfish"; Grey, *Tales of Southern Rivers*, 26.

2. "Long Key Fishing Camp—Improvements."

3. Rogers, "Standardized Motor Boats," 23.

4. Leitch, *Motor Boats and Boat Motors*, 199.

5. Rogers, "Standardized Motor Boats," 23–25.

6. Lester, "Sailfish on Light Tackle," 424.

7. Ibid., 426.

8. Sutton, *The Silver Kings of Aransas Pass*, 259.

9. Grey, *Tales of Fishes*, 88–89.

10. Ellsworth, "Cotton-Thread Angling," 248–53.

11. Ibid., 249.

Chapter 7. The Clientele

1. Smith, *FDR*, 205–7; Oshinsky, *Polio*, 24–28.

2. Smith, *FDR*, 205–7.

3. Ibid; Roosevelt, "Log of the Houseboat Larooco," in Franklin D. Roosevelt Presidential Library and Museum, Hyde Park, NY.

4. Henderson, "How about Those Crowns?"

5. *Long Key Fishing Club, Season 1934–35*, 22; "Gehrig Lands Sailfish," *New York Times*, March 9, 1934; "Lou Gehrig Gets Big Thrill from Huge Devil Fish," *Key West Citizen*, March 13, 1935, 4.

6. Richardson, *Wallace Stevens*; Brazeau, *Parts of a World*, xi–xii.

7. Stevens, *The Contemplated Spouse*, 343–46, 396; Brazeau, *Parts of a World*, 97–99.

8. *Long Key Fishing Club, Season 1934–35*, 7.

9. "Daisy Leiter Marries," *New York Times*, December 27, 1904; Wiltshire Council, "Wiltshire Community History."

10. ThePeerage.com, a genealogical survey of the peerage of Britain as well as the royal families of Europe, Person Page 4908; "Henry Molyneux Paget [Howard], 19th Earl of Suffolk," Cracroft's Peerage: The Complete Guide to the British Peerage & Baronetage, www.cracroftspeerage.co.uk/online/content/suffolk1603.htm.

11. "Law: Litigious Leiters," *Time*, July 26, 1937, www.time.com/time/printout/0,8816,758059,00.html.

12. "Interesting Women of the Nobility." The Alexander Palace Time Machine Discussion Forum, http://forum.alexanderpalace.org/index.php?action=printpage;topic=8984.0.

13. *Long Key Fishing Club, Season 1931–1932*, 18–19.

14. "Tropic Storm Struck Hard at Long Key," *Florida Times-Union* (Jacksonville), September 7, 1935, 5; Pat Duane, interviews by Thomas N. Knowles, 2010.

15. *Long Key Fishing Club, Season 1934–35*, 20–23.

16. Obituary, B. W. Crowninshield, *Boston Daily Globe*, April 24, 1953; "Harvard College—Class of 1894 Fiftieth Anniversary Report 1894–1944" (Norwood, MA: Plimpton Press, 1910), 122; Ferguson, *Cleopatra's Barge*, 242–43.

17. Grey, "The Bonefish Brigade," 135–46.

18. Obituary, "Thomas D. M. Cardeza, *New York Times*, June 7, 1952; obituary, "Mrs. Thomas Cardeza," *New York Times*, November 12, 1943, 21.

19. Hall, "Thomas Drake," 257.

20. Geller, *Titanic*, 70–74; "Life History for Charlotte Drake Martinez Cardeza," West Laurel Hill Cemetery—Bringhurst Funeral Home, Forever-Care.com.

21. Geller, *Titanic*, 7; "The Slaters Sail Away," *Muse*, newsletter of the Slater Memorial Museum, Fall 2006, 4; "Thomas Cardeza," Encyclopedia Titanica Message Board, www.encyclopedia-titanica.org/2-men-bribe-titanic-sailors-save-lives.html.

22. Obituary, "Mrs. J. W. Cardeza," *New York Times*, August 2, 1939.

23. *Long Key Fishing Club, Season 1934–35*, 22.

Chapter 8. The Staff

1. *Decisions of the Comptroller,* 94.

2. "Flagler's Cisterns Still Functioning," *Key West Citizen,* Dec. 7, 2011; *Stone & Webster Journal* 27 (October 1920): 20; "Key West Historic Hotels—Key West Florida Beach Hotel Resorts—Casa Marina," www.casamarinaresort.com/resort_history/.

3. *American Angler,* February 1921, 580; "Born to Their Profession," *Catskill Recorder* (Greene Co., N.Y.), June 5, 1931, 5; *Catskill Recorder* (Greene Co., N.Y.), December 3, 1920, 8.

4. Hamilton Wright, "Landing the Big Fellows off Florida Keys; Real Thrill When Barracuda Takes Hook," *Brooklyn (N.Y.) Daily Eagle,* Dec. 6, 1925, 2G.

5. *New York Times,* January 17, 1926.

6. Wert, *Hoover,* 195; "Mr. Hoover Got Big Sail Fish," *Huntsville Daily Times,* February 11, 1930, 3.

7. "Mr. Hoover in Florida," *Huntsville Daily Times,* February 10, 1930, 1; "The Presidency: Winter Vacation," *Time,* February 17, 1930.

8. Wert, *Hoover,* 112–13.

9. Reports of the Department of Commerce—1917 (Washington, D.C.: U.S. Government Printing Office, 1918), 250; Wert, *Hoover,* 195.

10. "The Presidency: Winter Vacation," *Time,* February 17, 1930; "Mr. Hoover Got Big Sail Fish," *Huntsville Daily Times,* February 11, 1930, 3; "The President Changed Mind," *Huntsville Daily Times,* February 12, 1930, 1, 10.

11. "Wily Sailfish Elude Hoover; Begins Trip to Washington," *Brooklyn (N.Y.) Daily Eagle,* February 16, 1930, A2; "The President Changed Mind," *Huntsville Daily Times,* February 12, 1930, 1; "Keenly Seek Angling Honor," *Huntsville Daily Times,* February 13, 1930, 10.

12. "The-Presidency: Holiday's End," *Time,* February 24, 1930.

13. Ibid.; *Long Key Fishing Club, Season 1934–35,* 22; *Catskill Recorder* (Greene Co., N.Y.), February 14, 1930, 9.

14. *U.S. Census of Population: 1920 Florida Federal Population Schedules: Monroe Co.*, Washington, D.C.: Bureau of the Census Microfilm Laboratory. (This is the only federal census enumerated at Long Key during the fishing camp's season and therefore the only one that lists the positions at the fishing camp when it was at full staff.)

15. *Catskill Recorder* (Greene Co., N.Y.), December 10, 1920; December 27, 1918; *Greene County Examiner-Recorder.* February 23, 1950, 6.

16. Pat Duane, interviews by Thomas N. Knowles, 2010.

17. Ibid.

18. *U.S. Census of Population: 1910 Florida Federal Population Schedules: Monroe Co.* Washington, D.C.: Bureau of the Census Microfilm Laboratory; *Catskill Recorder* (Greene Co., N.Y.), January 4, 1918.

19. *Catskill Recorder* (Greene Co., N.Y.), March 14, 1919; Pat Duane, interviews by Thomas N. Knowles, 2010; State of Florida 1935 Census.

Chapter 9. The Last Caretaker

1. Caemmerer, *The Houses of Key West*, 90–91.

2. "Abe Goldman, Local Auto Salesman, Said to Have Been Driver of Death Car," *Florida Times-Union*, March 23, 1922, 18.

3. Kathleen O'Connor, "A Nation of Red Men," The Phoenixmasonry Masonic Museum and Library, www.phoenixmasonry.org/masonicmuseum/fraternalism/red_men.htm.

4. "Order of Red Men of the State Convene Today," *Jacksonville Times-Union*, March 22, 1922, 1.

5. "Abe Goldman, Local Auto Salesman."

6. *Reports of the Secretary of State of Florida*; *Bradford County Telegraph*, March 31, 1922, 3.

7. Hogan, "Laryngeal Diphtheria"; Park and Williams, *Pathogenic Microörganisms*.

8. "Howard Jefferson Sawyer, Jr.," *Florida Death Index 1877–1939*, https://familysearch.org/pal:/MM9.1.2/MZD4-18K/p1.

9. Reports of the Secretary of State of Florida.

10. Pat Duane, interviews by Thomas N. Knowles, 2010.

Chapter 10. The Depression and the Good Life at Long Key

1. "Louis P. Schutt, Hotel Man, Dies," *New York Times*, July 1, 1933; 1920 United States Federal Census, http://archive.org/details/14thcensusofpopu225unit.

2. "Brief History of the Navy in Key West," in *Your Navy in Key West* (Lubbock, TX: Boone, 1972); "Key West under State Control—Passes into Hands of FERA in Rehabilitation Program," *Key West Citizen*, July 5, 1934, 1.

3. *Long Key Fishing Club, Season 1934–35*, 13–23; Fred Bradford, "Fishing Guide," *Miami Daily News*, December 29, 1934, 17.

4. "Edgewood Chemical Biological Center: History," www.ecbc.army.mil/about/this_month_in_history.htm.

5. Hamilton Wright, "Landing the Big Fellows off Florida Keys," *Brooklyn (N.Y.) Daily Eagle*, December 6, 1925.

6. Duma, "Edward vom Hofe."

7. Gillespie, "Fly Tyers of New Brunswick"; "Custom Fly Brooches: The Patterns," www.pairowoodies.com/james/fly-patterns.html.

8. *Long Key Fishing Club, Season 1934–35*, 3, 24–28; George Greenfield, "Wood, Field and Stream," *New York Times*, August 16, 1935.

9. Pat Duane to author, e-mail message, August 16, 2011.

10. Documents in archival file at the Jacksonville National Weather Service Station, 2004.

11. Pat Duane, interviews by Thomas N. Knowles, 2010.

Chapter 11. Hurricanes

1. "First Warning of Hurricane Issued in Jax," *Jacksonville Journal*, August 19, 1935, 1.

2. Unisys Weather: Hurricane/Tropical Data for the Atlantic, http://weather.unisys.com/hurricane/atlantic; *Monthly Weather Review* 58–63 (1930–35).

3. "Testimony of Ivan E. Tannehill," in *Florida Hurricane Disaster*, 183.

4. Carlton J. Corliss, interview by Edward Akin; Gallagher, *Florida's Great Ocean Railway*, 62–64.

5. "Testimony of Ivan E. Tannehill," in *Florida Hurricane Disaster*, 183–85. All advisories for the 1935 Labor Day hurricane are taken from this source.

6. "Reorganization of the Hurricane Warning Service," *Weather Bureau Topics and Personnel*, May 1935, U.S. Dept. of Agriculture, Weather Bureau, Washington, D.C., 125–27.

7. Pat Duane, interviews by Thomas N. Knowles, 2010.

8. Frankenfield, "The Hurricane in South Florida," 664–73.

9. "Testimony of Julius F. Stone, Jr.," in *Florida Hurricane Disaster*, 77–78; *Miami Herald*, September 2, 1935, 2.

10. *Miami Herald*, September 2, 1935, 2; *New York Times*. September 3, 1935, 3.

11. "Testimony of Ivan E. Tannehill," in *Florida Hurricane Disaster*, 190.

12. Pat Duane, interviews by Thomas N. Knowles, 2010.

13. Brady, *Last Train from Key West.*

Chapter 12. The Labor Day Hurricane

1. "Caretaker at Long Key Gives Storm Account," *Key West Citizen*, September 5, 1935, 1.

2. Duane, "Observer's Report."

3. James Duane to Walter J. Bennett, Senior Meteorologist, Weather Bureau, Jacksonville, FL, September 25, 1935, Archives of the National Weather Service Weather Forecast Office, Jacksonville, FL.

4. Duane, "Observer's Report."

5. "Survivor Tells about Storm at Long Key Camp," *Florida Keys Sun*, September 6, 1935, 1, 7.

6. Pat Duane, interviews by Thomas N. Knowles, 2010.

7. Duane, "Observer's Report."

8. "Caretaker at Long Key Gives Storm Account," 1.

9. Ibid.

10. Duane, "Observer's Report"; "Caretaker at Long Key Gives Storm Account," 1.

11. Kennedy to Chief, U. S. Weather Bureau, Washington, D.C., September 10, 1935, Archives of the National Weather Service Weather Forecast Office, Jacksonville, FL; Brady, *The Last Train from Key West*, 9.

12. "45-Mile Wind Is Key West Top," *Miami Daily News*, September 3, 1935, 5; "Key West Phone Lines Go Out," *Miami Daily News*, September 3, 1935, 5.

13. Pat Duane, interviews by Thomas N. Knowles, 2010.

Chapter 13. The Long Road Home

1. Duane, "Observer's Report"; "Survivor Tells about Storm at Long Key Camp," *Florida Keys Sun*, September 6, 1935, 1, 7.

2. "Survivor Tells about Storm at Long Key Camp," 1, 7.

3. Right of Way and Track Maps, Florida East Coast Railway Co., sheet 17.

4. Bethel, *First Overseas Highway to Key West, Florida*; "Reduction in Ferry Trips Will Be Made," *Key West Citizen*, April 30, 1935, 1.

5. Right of Way and Track Maps, Florida East Coast Railway Co., sheet 18.

6. "Case Aides' Report of General Conditions Observed on Upper Keys from Matecumbe to Key West," Florida Emergency Relief Administration (FERA) District 9 Headquarters, September 16, 1935, National Archives.

7. Right of Way and Track Maps, Florida East Coast Railway Co., sheet 19.

8. Stevenson, *Key Guide—1966*, 30.

9. Brigham, "Key Vaca, Part II," 39–45; State of Florida 1935 Census; *United States Coast Pilot 1936*, 285.

10. "Caretaker at Long Key Gives Storm Account," 1, 4; "Survivor Tells about Storm at Long Key Camp," 1, 7.

11. Pat Duane, interviews by Thomas N. Knowles, 2010.

Chapter 14. After the Storm

1. Audrey Williams and Col. George Ijams, "Report to the President," in *Florida Hurricane Disaster*, 437–41.

2. Conrad Hyning, "Statement dated April 28, 1936," in *Florida Hurricane Disaster*, 331–33.

3. "Wind, Water and Woe," National Affairs, *Time*, September 16, 1935, 12–14.

4. "Radio Head Tells of Yacht Broadcast *of Dixie* Rescue," *Miami Daily News*, September 8, 1935, 2.

5. "12 Dead Found at Marathon, Grassy Key by Rescue Craft," *Miami Daily News*, September 6, 1935, 1, 12.

6. Ibid; "Radio Head Tells of Yacht Broadcast of *Dixie* Rescue," 2.

7. Right of Way and Track Maps, Florida East Coast Railway Co., sheet 17.

8. "Radio Head Tells of Yacht Broadcast of *Dixie* Rescue," 2; *Monthly Weather Review* 63, no. 9 (September 1935): 270; W. F. McDonald. "Lowest Barometer Reading in the Florida Keys Storm of September 2, 1935," *Monthly Weather Review* 63, no. 10 (October 1935): 295.

9. Edith Chesser Hancock, interviews by Tom Knowles, 2009. Mrs. Hancock was a resident of Pigeon Key during the 1935 Labor Day hurricane. Pat Duane, interviews by Thomas N. Knowles, 2010.

10. Pat Duane, interviews by Knowles, 2010.

11. Duane to Ernest Carson, Meteorologist-in-Charge, Miami Weather Bureau, Miami, FL, September 14, 1935, Archives of the National Weather Service Weather Forecast Office, Jacksonville, FL; Pat Duane, interviews by Knowles, 2010.

12. Pat Duane, interviews by Knowles, 2010.

13. Duane to Walter J. Bennett, Senior Meteorologist, Weather Bureau, Jacksonville, FL, September 25, 1935, Archives of the National Weather Service Weather Forecast Office, Jacksonville, FL.

14. Max Mayer to Walter Chute, director, Shedd Aquarium, September 23, 1935, John G. Shedd Aquarium Archives; "The Florida Hurricane," *Railway Age* 100, no. 10 (March 7, 1936): 385.

Epilogue

1. Pat Duane, interviews by Thomas N. Knowles, 2010.

2. Ibid.; Annie Jaggers, *Billy Freeman,* 234–37.

3. *Flagler's Florida,* The Whitehall Society of the Henry Morrison Flagler Museum, The *Palm Beach Post,* and the School District of Palm Beach County, 2008, 28, http://interactive.sun-sentinel.com/services/newspaper/education/nie/curriculum/Flag_tab.pdf.

4. *St. Augustine Evening Record,* May 20, 1913.

5. "Born in the Business," *Catskill Recorder* (Greene Co., N.Y.), February 11, 1927; "Born to Their Profession," *Catskill Recorder* (Greene Co., N.Y.), June 5, 1931.

6. "Legend of the Peabody Ducks," The Peabody-Memphis, Tennessee, www.peabodymemphis.com/peabody-ducks/.7. "Louis P. Schutt, Hotel Man, Dies," *New York Times,* July 1, 1933; "Seven Planes Arrived Here This Morning," *Key West Citizen,* January 14, 1935.

8. Federal Writers' Project, Work Projects Administration, State of Florida, *Florida—A Guide to the Southernmost State,* 332; "Colorful Sugar Loaf Key Now Being Made into Fishing Paradise for Rich Anglers," *Miami Daily News,* January 7, 1940, 9A.

9. Long Key Fishing Club booklets for seasons 1931–35, published annually by the Long Key Fishing Club; "Bruton," in *A History of the County of Somerset,* vol. 7, *Bruton, Horethorne and Norton Ferris Hundreds* (1999), 18–42, www.british-history.ac.uk/report.aspx?compid=18733&strquery=Leiter.

10. "BBC—WW2 People's War—The Earl and the Secretary," www.bbc.co.uk/print/ww2peopleswar/stories/43/a3924443.shtml.

11. "Margaret Lady Howard Dies; Dowager Countess of Suffolk," *New York Times,* March 6, 1968.

12. "Life History for Charlotte Drake Martinez Cardeza," Forever-Care.com; *Jefferson Medical College Alumni Bulletin* 3, no. 2 (June 1941), Thomas Jefferson University, Jefferson Digital Commons, 12–14.

13. Robinson, *Iron Horse*; "Gehrig, 'Iron Man' of Baseball, Dies at the Age of 37," *New York Times,* June 3, 1941.

14. Baker, ed., *Ernest Hemingway*, 438–40; Matthew Billingsley, "Wallace Stevens," in *Biographies by Claim to Fame*, Pennsylvania Center for the Book, Penn State University, May 17, 2013, http://pabook.libraries.psu.edu/palitmap/fame.html.

15. Ferguson, *Cleopatra's Barge*, 243.

16. Gruber, *Zane Grey*, 225.

17. "The Florida Hurricane," *Railway Age* 100, no. 10 (March 7, 1936): 385; Kendrick, *Florida Trails to Turnpikes*, 139; Hopkins, "The Development of the Overseas Highway," 53, 55.

18. "Celebration Marks Completion of Link Spanning Last Gap," *Miami Daily News*, March 29, 1938, 1; Lovering, 21–22.

19. "Brief History of the Navy in Key West," 5; Hopkins, "The Development of the Overseas Highway," 53, 55.

20. Heinlein, "Key West Search for Fresh Water," 4–10.

21. Ibid.

22. Right of Way and Track Maps, Florida East Coast Railway Co., sheet 17; "Long Key Fishing Camp Brings Price of $35,000," *Key West Citizen*, June 29, 1945.

23. Deed, Official Records of Monroe County, Florida, book 228, page 563; "Long Key State Park Unit Management Plan Approved September 1, 2004," State of Florida Department of Environmental Protection, Division of Recreation and Parks, 1.

24. "Layton city, Florida Census 2010 Results," United States Census Bureau, http://factfinder2.census.gov.

25. Karl D. Borglum, Property Appraiser, Monroe County, Florida, www.mcpafl.org.

26. Reiger, *The Best of Zane Grey*, 134–35.

Appendix

1. Dunn and Miller, *Atlantic Hurricanes*, 61–62.

2. U.S. Army Corps of Engineers, "Florida Keys, Chart of Hurricane of Sept. 2, 1935."

3. "Case Aides' Report of General Conditions Observed on Upper Keys from Matecumbe to Key West," Florida Emergency Relief Administration (FERA) District 9 Headquarters, September 16, 1935, www.keyshistory.org/35-hurr-Aides-report.html; *Florida Hurricane Disaster*, report by E. R. Lowe on pages 350–51, and annotations on map between pages 182 and 183.

4. Dean, *Lighthouses of the Florida Keys*, 150; U.S. Army Corps of Engineers, "Florida Keys, Chart of Hurricane of Sept. 2, 1935.

Bibliography

Baker, Carlos, ed., *Ernest Hemingway: Selected Letters 1917–1961*. New York: Scribner, 1981.

Bethel, Rod. *First Overseas Highway to Key West, Florida*. Oviedo, FL: Mickler's Floridiana, 1989.

Braden, Susan R. *The Architecture of Leisure: The Florida Resort Hotels of Henry Flagler and Henry Plant*. Gainesville: University Press of Florida, 2002.

Brady, Doris L. *The Last Train from Key West*. Self-published, 1995.

Brazeau, Peter. *Parts of a World: Wallace Stevens Remembered*. New York: Random House, 1983.

Brigham, Florence S. "Key Vaca, Part II; Modern Phase." *Tequesta* 1, no. 18 (1958).

Bryce, James. *The American Commonwealth*. Vol. 2. London: Macmillan, 1889.

Caemmerer, Alex. *The Houses of Key West*. Sarasota, FL: Pineapple Press, 1992.

Call, Henry L. *The Concentration of Wealth*. Boston: Chandler, 1907.

Chance, Elizabeth Williams. Interview of a survivor of the 1935 Labor Day Hurricane by Thomas N. Knowles, February 13, 1998. Middleburg, FL.

Chandler, David Leon. *Henry Flagler: The Astonishing Life and Times of the Visionary Robber Baron Who Founded Florida*. New York: Macmillan, 1986.

Corliss, Carlton J. "Building the Overseas Railway to Key West." *Tequesta* 1, no. 13 (1953): 3–21.

———. "Henry M. Flagler: Railroad Builder." *Florida Historical Quarterly* 38, no. 3 (January 1960): 195–205.

———. Interview by Edward Akin. University of Florida Oral History Project. April 28, 1973, and October 6, 1973, http://ufdc.ufl.edu/?b=UF00005577&v=00001.

Dean, Love. *Lighthouses of the Florida Keys*. Key West, FL: Historic Florida Keys Foundation, 1992.

Decisions of the Comptroller of the Treasury. Vol. 24, *Fiscal Year 1917–1918*. Washington, D.C.: U.S. Government Printing Office, 1918.

Dement, Jeff. "Species Spotlight: Atlantic Sailfish." www.littoralsociety.org/userfiles/doccenter/Species%20Spotlight%20Atlantic%20Sailfish.pdf.

Dodge, Charles Richards. "Subtropical Florida." *Scribner's Magazine*, March 1894, 345–62.

Duane, James E. "Observer's Report on Hurricane of September 2nd, 1935." Typed report delivered to Gerald Kennedy, Key West Weather Bureau, September 1935. Archives of the National Weather Service Weather Forecast Office, Jacksonville, FL.

Duma, Stefan. "Edward vom Hofe, Part II." www.antiquetackleobserver.com/2010/01/02/edward-vom-hofe-pt-ii/.

Dunn, Gordon E., and Banner I Miller. *Atlantic Hurricanes.* Baton Rouge: Louisiana State University Press, 1960.

Ellsworth, Fred Bradford. "The Story of Cotton-Thread Angling." Pt. 1. *American Angler*, October 1920, 248–53.

Federal Writers' Project, Work Projects Administration, State of Florida. *Florida—A Guide to the Southernmost State.* New York: Oxford University Press, 1999.

Ferguson, David L. *Cleopatra's Barge: The Crowninshield Story.* Boston: Little, Brown, 1976.

Florida East Coast Hotel Co. Map of Part of Long Key, 1923 Correction & Tracing.

Florida Hurricane Disaster: Hearings before the Committee On World War Veterans' Legislation, House of Representatives, Seventy-Fourth Congress, Second Session on H.R. 9486. Washington, D.C.: U.S. Government Printing Office, 1936.

Frankenfield, H. C. "The Hurricane in South Florida." *Monthly Weather Review.* www.aoml.noaa.gov/general/lib/lib1/nhclib/mwreviews/1919.pdf.

Gallagher, Dan. *Florida's Great Ocean Railway: Building the Key West Extension.* Sarasota, FL: Pineapple Press, 2003.

Geller, Judith B. *Titanic: Women and Children First.* New York: Norton, 1998.

Gillespie, Dewey H., and Walter Francis Kitchen. "Fly Tyers of New Brunswick." www.flyfishingnb.com/.

Graham, Thomas. "Henry M. Flagler's Hotel Ponce de Leon." "Florida Theme" issue of *Journal of Decorative and Propaganda Arts* 23 (1998): 96–111.

Grey, Zane. "The Amberjack of Sombrero Reef." *Field and Stream,* February 1913, 1113–1119.

———. "The Bonefish Brigade." In *The Best of Zane Grey, Outdoorsman: Hunting and Fishing Tales,* edited by George Reiger, 135–46. Mechanicsburg, PA: Stackpole, 1992.

———. *Tales of Fishes.* New York: Grosset and Dunlap, 1919.

———. *Tales of Southern Rivers.* New York: Harper and Brothers, 1924.

Gruber, Frank. *Zane Grey: A Biography.* New York: New American Library, 1970.

Hall, Henry, ed. "Thomas Drake." In *America's Successful Men of Affairs: An Encyclopedia of Contemporaneous Biography,* 2:257. Tribune Assn., 1896.

Heilner, Van Campen. *Adventures in Angling.* Cincinnati: Stewart Kidd, 1922.

Heinlein, Carston. "Key West Search for Fresh Water—Part Three." *Florida Keys Sea Heritage Journal* 16, no. 3 (Spring 2006): 1, 3–16.

Henderson, Wayne. "How About Those Crowns?" *Petroleum Collectibles Monthly,* June 2001. www.pcmpublishing.com/articles/22.html.

Hogan, John F., M.D. "Laryngeal Diphtheria." *JAMA: The Journal of the American Medical Association* 77 (1921): 662–64.

Hopkins, Alice. "The Development of the Overseas Highway." *Tequesta* 86, no. 1 (1986): 53–55.

Iardella, C. T., and F. W. Dorr. Extracts from their reports of April 1858 on the survey of the keys south of Key Largo. Published as *Executive Documents of the House of Representatives of the United States, Second Session, Thirty-Fifth Congress*, vol. 1. Washington, D.C.: James P. Steedman, Printer, 1859.

Jaggers, Annie. *Billy Freeman, Florida Keys Sheriff.* Key West: Cayo, 2000.

Josephson, Matthew. *The Robber Barons: The Great American Capitalists 1861–1901.* New York: Harcourt, Brace, 1934.

Kendrick, Baynard. *Florida Trails to Turnpikes.* Gainesville: University of Florida Press, 1964.

Knetsch, Joe. "The Business System of Henry Flagler." *El Escribano* 40 (2003): 68–91.

LeFèvre, Edwin. "Flagler and Florida." *Everybody's Magazine*, February 1910, 168–86.

Leitch, Albert Clark. *Motor Boats and Boat Motors.* New York: Henley, 1920.

Lester, C. H. "Sailfish on Light Tackle." *American Angler*, January 1921, 424–27.

Long Key Fishing Club, Season 1931–1932. Booklet. Long Key, FL: Long Key Fishing Club, 1931.

Long Key Fishing Club, Season 1934–35. Booklet. Long Key, FL: Long Key Fishing Club, 1934.

Lovering, Frank W. *A Hurricane Between.* St. Augustine, FL: Frank Lovering, 1946.

Mannering, Mitchell. "The Hidden Wealth of Florida." *National Magazine*, April 1910, 136–46.

Moffett, Samuel E. "Henry Morrison Flagler." *Cosmopolitan*, August 1902, 416–19.

Mueller, Edward A. "The FEC Steamship Company." *Tequesta* 1, no. 36 (1976).

Munroe, Kirk. *Canoemates.* New York: Harper, 1905.

Oshinsky, David M. *Polio: An American Story.* New York: Oxford University Press, 2005.

Paine, Ralph D. "Over the Florida Keys by Rail." *Everybody's Magazine*, February 1908, 153.

Park, William Hallock, and Anna Williams. *Pathogenic Microörganisms.* With Charles Krumwiede. 7th ed. New York: Lea and Febiger, 1920.

Perrine, Henry. "Successive Crops of Cocoons in Tropical Florida." Letter to the editor. *Farmers' Register* 7, no. 9 (1839).

Phillips, Kevin. *The Politics of Rich and Poor.* New York: Harper Perennial, 1991.

Reiger, George, ed. *The Best of Zane Grey, Outdoorsman: Hunting and Fishing Tales.* Mechanicsburg, PA: Stackpole, 1992.

Reports of the Secretary of State of the State of Florida for 1921–1922 through 1925–1926. State of Florida Archives.

Reynolds, Charles B. *The Standard Guide—Florida.* New York: Foster and Reynolds, 1921.

———. *The Standard Guide—St. Augustine.* St. Augustine, FL: E. H. Reynolds, 1890.

Richardson, Joan. *Wallace Stevens: The Early Years, 1879–1923.* New York: Beech Tree, 1986.

Right of Way and Track Maps, Florida East Coast Railway Co., Corrected to Dec.

31, 1927, with annotations of track position and condition after the 1935 Labor Day hurricane. A blueprint copy is held by the Monroe County Public Library, Key West, FL.

Robinson, Ray. *Iron Horse: Lou Gehrig in His Time*. New York: Norton, 1990.

Robison, T. Ralph. "Henry Perrine, Pioneer Horticulturist of Florida." *Tequesta* 1, no. 2 (August 1942): 16–24.

Rockefeller, John D. *Random Reminiscences of Men and Events*. New York: Doubleday, Page, 1909.

Rogers, William B., Jr. "Standardized Motor Boats for Florida Resort." *Motor Boat*, January 25, 1920, 23–25.

Saunders, William H. "The Wreck of Houseboat No. 4 October 1906." *Tequesta* 1, no. 19 (1959).

Schene, Michael. "Indian Key." *Tequesta* 1, no. 36 (1976).

Smith, Jean Edward. *FDR*. New York: Random House, 2008.

Staats, Luther Edward. "The Transformation of the Florida East Coast." *Bankers' Magazine*, January-June 1909, 258–64.

State of Florida 1935 Census. Monroe County—Precinct 8. State of Florida Archives. Tallahassee, FL.

Stevens, Wallace. *The Contemplated Spouse: The Letters of Wallace Stevens to Elsie*. Edited by J. Donald Blount. Columbia: University of South Carolina Press, 2006.

Stevenson, George B. *Key Guide—1966*. Tavernier, FL: George B. Stevenson, 1965.

Sutton, Richard L. *The Silver Kings of Aransas Pass and Other Stories*. Kansas City, MO: Brown-White, 1937.

Tannehill, I. R. *The Hurricane*. U.S. Dept. of Agriculture, Misc. Publication No. 197. Washington, D.C.: U.S. Government Printing Office, 1934.

U.S. Army Corps of Engineers. "Florida Keys, Chart of Hurricane of Sept. 2, 1935 Including Profile of Florida East Coast Railway And Other Data." U.S. Engineer Sub-Office, Miami Beach, Florida, File No. 3-16-10,409, October 1935.

United States Coast Pilot 1936. U.S. Dept. of Commerce. Washington, D.C.: U.S. Government Printing Office, 1936.

Wells, L. Stewart, ed. "Council of Fire." *Outing Magazine*, March 1918, 414–15.

Wert, Hal Elliott. *Hoover: The Fishing President*. Mechanicsburg, PA: Stackpole, 2005.

Wiltshire Council. "Wiltshire Community History." http://history.wiltshire.gov.uk/community/getcom.php?id=48.

Index

Thomas Neil Knowles is a former naval officer and a retired university administrator who enjoys researching and writing about historical subjects, especially those involving the Florida Keys. Born and raised in Key West, he is a fourth-generation Conch whose ancestors moved from the Bahamas to the island in the mid-1800s. He is the author of *Category 5: The 1935 Labor Day Hurricane* and various historical articles.